# THE BENEFIT OF DOUBT

A Pillar of the Justice System

**NARAYANA SWAMY .R**

Advocate, High Court Of Karnataka

NARAYANASAMY.R

**Copyright © 2024** All rights reserved.

No part of this publication may be reproduced, stored in a retrieval system, or transmitted in any form or by any means electronic, mechanical, photocopying, recording, or otherwise without the prior written permission of the publisher.

# Acknowledgements and Dedication

This book is lovingly dedicated to the memories and unwavering support of my family, who have been my greatest sources of strength and inspiration.

To my late father, **Rangappa M.K.**, and my mother, **Lakshminarasamma** your values and guidance have been the foundation of my life and work. This book is a tribute to the resilience, wisdom, and integrity you instilled in me.

To my brother, **Shivashankara** thank you for always standing by my side, offering encouragement and support in countless ways. Your belief in me has meant more than words can express.

And to my beloved wife, **Gowthami M.N** your patience, love, and encouragement have been my anchor through every step of this journey. This book would not have been possible without your strength and unwavering support.

**With heartfelt gratitude**, I dedicate this work to each of you.

# Preface

In the world of law, where the stakes are high and lives are forever changed by verdicts, one principle stands as the very foundation of justice the *Benefit of Doubt*. It is the silent guardian of fairness, ensuring that justice is not swayed by emotion, prejudice, or assumption. This book, *The Benefit of Doubt: A Pillar of the Justice System*, delves into this powerful yet often misunderstood concept, unraveling its complexities and exploring its role in shaping the course of legal proceedings.

Why does the law demand that guilt be proven beyond a reasonable doubt? What does this principle truly mean for those accused of crimes, and how does it protect the innocent? These are the central questions that this book seeks to answer, taking you on a journey through the heart of criminal justice.

For centuries, the *Benefit of Doubt* has served as the cornerstone of criminal law, ensuring that no person is unjustly convicted. It is a shield that prevents wrongful convictions, a reminder that in the realm of justice, certainty is a rare commodity. Every court case hinges on this principle, as judges and juries navigate the delicate balance between evidence, testimony, and the ever-present possibility of doubt.

But what happens when doubt becomes the deciding factor? How does it shape verdicts? Can the innocent sometimes suffer as a result of too much doubt? Through real-life case studies, landmark rulings, and deep legal analysis, this book sheds light on these critical questions. Each chapter explores different facets of this principle from its role in ensuring a fair trial to its ethical dilemmas and offers readers a clear understanding of its profound impact on the justice system.

In *The Benefit of Doubt: A Pillar of the Justice System*, you will discover:

- **How the legal system defines and applies "reasonable doubt"** to protect the rights of the accused.
- **The powerful ethical dilemmas** faced by judges, lawyers, and juries when doubt stands between justice and the truth.
- **Real case studies and landmark rulings** that illustrate how the principle of doubt has shaped both acquittals and convictions.
- **The future of the principle** in an evolving legal landscape, and how it might adapt to new challenges in the pursuit of justice.

This book is not only for law students or legal professionals it is for anyone who believes in the power of fairness and truth. Whether you're seeking to understand the complexities of criminal law or simply curious about how justice works behind closed courtroom doors, *The Benefit of Doubt: A Pillar of the Justice System* will guide you through the maze of legal reasoning with clarity and insight.

As you turn the pages, you will be drawn into the stories of individuals whose lives were shaped by this principle. You'll gain a new appreciation for the delicate balance that must be maintained between conviction and doubt, and you'll see how the benefit of doubt serves as the pillar that upholds the integrity of our legal system.

**T**he pursuit of justice is never straightforward. But with the *Benefit of Doubt*, we are reminded that the search for truth is always a journey one that requires patience, careful consideration, and, above all, a commitment to fairness. Join me as we explore this fundamental principle of law, and discover how doubt, far from being a weakness, is the ultimate safeguard of justice.

**NARAYANASWAMY.R**

**Advocate & Author.**

## Why This Book?

**I**n every courtroom, at every trial, the most critical question isn't just "Did the accused commit the crime?" but rather, "Can the guilt of the accused be proven beyond a reasonable doubt?" This simple yet profound question is the cornerstone of our justice system the *Benefit of Doubt*. It's a principle that protects the innocent, challenges the powerful, and ensures fairness is at the heart of every legal process. But how often do we truly understand the depth and significance of this fundamental concept?

*The Benefit of Doubt: A Pillar of the Justice System* is more than just a book about law. It's an exploration of the very essence of justice and fairness that guides our legal system. In this book, we will delve deep into the mechanics of reasonable doubt its significance, its challenges, and its implications in criminal trials. By the end of this book, you will not only gain a profound understanding of the *Benefit of Doubt* but also develop a new appreciation for the intricate balance that our legal system strikes in the pursuit of truth.

But why should *you* read this book?

1. **To Understand the Foundation of Criminal Justice**
   At the core of criminal law lies the principle of reasonable doubt. This book will help you understand why this concept is not just a technicality but a pillar that upholds fairness in the legal process. Whether you're a legal professional, a student, or someone with a deep interest in justice, understanding how reasonable doubt works is critical to understanding how the law operates.

2. **To See the Human Side of Legal Principles**
   While law often feels abstract and impersonal, at its heart, it is about real people real lives affected by verdicts. This book takes you beyond the legal jargon and connects you with the human element behind every trial. You'll discover how reasonable doubt can affect not just verdicts but the lives of the accused, the victims, and their families. By reading real-life case studies and landmark rulings, you will witness the power of doubt in shaping the course of justice.
3. **To Uncover the Ethical Dilemmas That Shape Verdicts**
   Doubt isn't always as clear-cut as it seems. Sometimes, the line between reasonable and unreasonable doubt is thin, and the consequences of this ambiguity are profound. This book explores the ethical dilemmas judges and juries face when doubt shadows their decision-making. What happens when the benefit of doubt protects the guilty? What happens when it fails to shield the innocent? By tackling these questions, this book invites you to reflect on the very nature of justice itself.
4. **To Learn From Landmark Legal Cases**
   Throughout history, the *Benefit of Doubt* has played a pivotal role in some of the most significant legal cases. In this book, we examine these landmark rulings and analyze how courts have interpreted and applied this principle in real-life situations. By learning from these cases, you will gain a clearer understanding of how the *Benefit of Doubt* can make or break a case.
5. **To Explore the Future of Justice**
   The legal system is constantly evolving, and so too is our understanding of doubt and its role in the judicial process.

As new challenges and complexities arise, it's important to consider how the *Benefit of Doubt* will adapt to meet these demands. In this book, we explore the future of this principle, providing insights into how it might shape the justice system in years to come.

6. **For Those Who Seek Justice in its Purest Form**
This book is for anyone who believes in justice not as an abstract concept but as a living, breathing force that must be fought for and understood. If you're passionate about fairness, truth, and the pursuit of justice, *The Benefit of Doubt* will give you the tools to better understand and appreciate how these ideals manifest in the courtroom.

Whether you're a legal expert, a law student, or simply someone who believes in the importance of fairness in society, this book offers a comprehensive and thought-provoking exploration of one of the most fundamental principles of law. Through a mix of case studies, ethical analysis, and in-depth legal exploration, it provides an engaging and insightful look at how the *Benefit of Doubt* plays a crucial role in shaping justice.

*The Benefit of Doubt* is not just a principle it is the heart of a justice system that has been crafted over centuries to protect the innocent and ensure that fairness prevails. By reading this book, you will not only gain a deeper understanding of this cornerstone of the legal system but also witness how doubt, in its truest sense, is a powerful force for good.

So, why read this book? Because in a world where justice often hangs in the balance, understanding the *Benefit of Doubt* could be the key to unlocking the very future of fairness in the legal system. Dive in, and discover how doubt, when applied with wisdom and care, is not a weakness but a pillar that holds up the very foundation of justice.

# TABLE OF CONTENTS

Chapter-1 ............................................................. 14

The Benefit of Doubt: A Shield of Justice ........ 14

Chapter-2 ............................................................. 18

The Principle of Reasonable Doubt: The Cornerstone of Fair Justice ............................... 18

Chapter-3 ............................................................. 22

Legal Maxims That Define Justice: Timeless Pillars of Fairness ............................................. 22

Chapter-4 ............................................................. 26

The Anatomy of Doubt: How It Shapes Verdicts ............................................................................ 26

Chapter-5 ............................................................. 31

Practical Application in Real Cases: How the Benefit of Doubt Shapes Justice ...................... 31

Chapter-6 ............................................................. 36

Key Elements That Raise Doubt: The Cracks in the Armor of Conviction ................................. 36

Chapter-7 ............................................................. 41

The Role of Cross-Examination: The Battlefield of Truth ................................................. 41

Chapter-8 ................................................................. 46

Landmark Judgments: The Benefit of Doubt in Action ................................................................. 46

Chapter-9 ................................................................. 51

The Ethical Dilemma: When Doubt Saves the Guilty ................................................................. 51

Chapter-10 ............................................................... 55

Safeguarding the Innocent: The Way Forward 55

Chapter-11 ............................................................... 60

The Global Perspective: The Benefit of Doubt Across Borders ................................................... 60

Chapter-12 ............................................................... 66

Criticism and Controversy: The Shadows of Doubt ................................................................. 66

Chapter-13 ............................................................... 71

The Lawyer's Toolkit: Arguing for the Benefit of Doubt ................................................................. 71

Chapter-14 ............................................................... 77

Conclusion: A Pillar of Justice and Humanity. 77

Chapter-15 .................................................................. 82

Annexures ................................................................... 82

Annexures ................................................................... 83

Glossary of Legal Terms............................................. 83

Landmark Case Summaries ...................................... 84

  1. Kali Ram v. State of Himachal Pradesh (1973 AIR 2773) ..................................................................... 84

  2. Sharad Birdhichand Sarda v. State of Maharashtra (1984 AIR 1622)...................................... 85

  3. State of U.P. v. Krishna Gopal and Another (1988 AIR 2154) ..................................................... 86

  4. Bhim Singh v. State of Haryana (2002 AIR 437) ........................................................................... 87

  5. Narendra Singh v. State of M.P. (2004 AIR 26) .................................................................................. 87

Legal Provisions and References ...................... 88

Final Thoughts ................................................... 90

# Chapter-1

# The Benefit of Doubt: A Shield of Justice

# The Benefit of Doubt: A Shield of Justice

Imagine being accused of a crime you didn't commit. Your reputation, freedom, and future hang by a thread. What if the evidence against you is unclear or contradictory? This is where the *benefit of doubt* becomes your shield, protecting you from injustice. In criminal law, this principle ensures that only the truly guilty are punished while safeguarding the innocent from wrongful convictions. But how does it work, and why is it so crucial?

This chapter takes you to the heart of justice itself, unraveling the concept of the benefit of doubt a powerful yet delicate principle that serves as the cornerstone of fair trials and human rights.

### Introduction: The Foundation of Justice

Justice isn't just about punishing the guilty; it's about ensuring no innocent person suffers unjustly. This idea forms the bedrock of criminal law. The concept of *benefit of doubt* reflects the legal system's commitment to fairness, where suspicion alone is never enough to convict someone.

In this chapter, we'll explore the origins, evolution, and significance of this principle in ensuring the delicate balance between guilt and innocence. Why do courts insist on proof *beyond a reasonable doubt*? What makes this principle indispensable to justice systems worldwide? These answers lie ahead.

## What Is the Benefit of Doubt?

The *benefit of doubt* is the ultimate safety net in criminal justice. It ensures that no person is condemned based on uncertainty or speculation. Simply put, if there's any reasonable doubt about the guilt of an accused, the court must acquit them.

Think of it as a filter, separating true guilt from mere accusation. Without this safeguard, innocent individuals would face grave injustices, and trust in the legal system would crumble. The benefit of doubt isn't a loophole it's the system's way of upholding its highest ideals.

## Why It Matters in Criminal Law

Criminal trials aren't just battles of evidence they're battles for truth. In this high-stakes arena, even the smallest doubt can mean the difference between freedom and imprisonment, or worse, life and death.

1. **Protecting the Innocent:** History is filled with cases where innocent lives were ruined due to hasty convictions. The benefit of doubt ensures justice errs on the side of caution.
2. **Ensuring Accountability:** By demanding proof beyond doubt, it forces investigators and prosecutors to build stronger, more credible cases.
3. **Maintaining Trust:** A justice system that punishes based on uncertainty risks losing public confidence. The benefit of doubt upholds the system's integrity and fairness.

As you turn the pages, you'll discover how this principle has been applied in real cases, sometimes saving lives and other times sparking heated debates. This is not just about legal theory it's about justice in action.

# Chapter-2

# The Principle of Reasonable Doubt: The Cornerstone of Fair Justice

# The Principle of Reasonable Doubt: The Cornerstone of Fair Justice

**P**icture yourself standing trial for a crime you didn't commit. The world seems to be against you, and the stakes couldn't be higher. Would you want the court to decide your fate based on mere assumptions? This is where the **principle of reasonable doubt** emerges as your greatest ally. It's not just a legal standard it's a lifeline, ensuring fairness and protecting the innocent from wrongful conviction.

This chapter unpacks the profound significance of reasonable doubt, revealing how it has become the foundation of justice systems worldwide and how it continues to shape verdicts in criminal trials.

**Presumption of Innocence: A Sacred Rule**

The presumption of innocence isn't just a legal phrase it's the heartbeat of criminal justice. Imagine walking into a courtroom, accused of a crime. This rule means that until proven guilty, the system treats you as innocent. The burden of proof lies entirely with the prosecution.

Why is this principle sacred? Because it levels the playing field. In a world where accusations can ruin lives, the presumption of innocence is a shield against prejudice, ensuring no one is treated unfairly before evidence is weighed. It's a promise from the justice system: *We will not condemn you without proof.*

This rule isn't just theoretical. It manifests in every courtroom, reminding judges, lawyers, and jurors that the cost of convicting the innocent is too high a price for society to pay.

## How Courts Interpret "Reasonable Doubt"

What exactly does "reasonable doubt" mean? Is it a feeling, a calculation, or something else entirely? Courts define reasonable doubt as a doubt based on reason and logic not mere suspicion or emotional reactions. It's a standard that requires clear, convincing evidence to convict an accused.

But here's the catch: Reasonable doubt isn't about absolute certainty. Human judgment is fallible, and courts acknowledge this. Instead, they demand evidence so compelling that any logical person would conclude guilt. If even a shred of doubt exists that a reasonable mind cannot ignore, the benefit goes to the accused.

## The Courtroom in Action

- **In Theory:** A judge tells the jury to rely on their rational judgment, asking, "Are you sure of the accused's guilt? If not, the doubt is reasonable."
- **In Practice:** A defense lawyer exposes gaps in the prosecution's case, showing how evidence fails to rule out every possibility of innocence.

Through landmark judgments and real-world scenarios, this chapter explores how courts navigate the complexities of reasonable doubt, ensuring justice doesn't falter. You'll see why this principle is more than just a legal safeguard it's the soul of a fair trial system.

# Chapter-3

# Legal Maxims That Define Justice: Timeless Pillars of Fairness

# Legal Maxims That Define Justice: Timeless Pillars of Fairness

Legal systems across the world are built on profound principles timeless truths that serve as the foundation of justice. Among these are two legal maxims that have stood as unwavering guides, shaping the philosophy of fairness and protecting individuals from the weight of wrongful convictions. These principles are not mere words; they are the very essence of humanity in law.

This chapter dives deep into two of the most compelling legal maxims, their origins, significance, and how they continue to influence the modern justice system.

### "Innocent Until Proven Guilty": The Golden Rule

Imagine a world where you are treated as guilty the moment you are accused. The devastation of such a system is unfathomable. That's why the maxim *"Innocent Until Proven Guilty"* exists it's a shield that protects individuals from the dangers of false accusations.

### The Philosophy Behind the Maxim

At its core, this principle ensures that the burden of proof lies with the accuser, not the accused. The accused does not have to prove their innocence; instead, the prosecution must establish guilt beyond a reasonable doubt. This rule upholds fairness by preventing hasty judgments fueled by bias or prejudice.

## In Action: The Courtroom Dynamics

- A defense lawyer uses this maxim as their first line of argument: "My client stands innocent unless the prosecution proves otherwise."
- Judges remind jurors that the accused enters the trial with the presumption of innocence, urging them to weigh evidence without preconceived notions.

This sacred rule has not only saved countless innocent lives but also strengthened the moral fabric of the legal system, ensuring fairness prevails over mere suspicion.

## "Better Ten Guilty Escape Than One Innocent Suffer": The Moral Dilemma

Is it acceptable to punish an innocent person to ensure that the guilty are not let go? This maxim, often attributed to English jurist William Blackstone, boldly answers: *No*.

## The Principle in Perspective

This maxim reflects the value of individual liberty and human dignity. It acknowledges the devastating impact of a wrongful conviction not just on the individual but on society's faith in justice. While it may seem controversial to let the guilty escape, the cost of punishing even one innocent person is deemed too high.

**Real-Life Implications**

- **The Ethical Debate:** Critics argue this principle allows criminals to escape accountability. Supporters, however, see it as a necessary trade-off to protect the innocent.
- **Courtroom Examples:** Defense lawyers skillfully exploit gaps in the prosecution's evidence, creating reasonable doubt to ensure no innocent person is wrongly convicted.

**Why These Maxims Matter Today**

In an era of instant judgments and social media trials, these maxims serve as crucial reminders of what true justice entails. They urge us to pause, reflect, and ensure that fairness and reason guide our decisions.

As you explore this chapter, you'll uncover stories of how these principles have shaped landmark rulings, safeguarded lives, and sparked intense debates. Are these maxims foolproof? Can they stand the test of modern challenges? The answers lie ahead in this captivating journey through the soul of justice.

NARAYANASAMY.R

# Chapter-4

# The Anatomy of Doubt: How It Shapes Verdicts

# The Anatomy of Doubt: How It Shapes Verdicts

Every courtroom is a battleground of evidence, arguments, and emotions, but at its heart lies a silent yet powerful force: **doubt**. Doubt is what keeps justice honest, ensuring that decisions are not rushed, evidence is scrutinized, and truth is pursued relentlessly. But not all doubts are created equal. Some are born from logic and reason, while others stem from conjecture and bias.

This chapter dissects doubt, unraveling its nuances and showing how it transforms the outcomes of criminal trials. By the end, you'll understand how the justice system distinguishes between valid doubts that demand acquittal and baseless doubts that should be ignored.

### Identifying Reasonable vs. Unreasonable Doubt

Not every question or uncertainty raised during a trial constitutes reasonable doubt. Courts demand that doubt be grounded in rationality and evidence not wild speculation. But where do we draw the line?

### Reasonable Doubt: The Shield of Justice

Reasonable doubt is a doubt that arises logically after examining the evidence and weighing the arguments. It's the nagging question in a juror's mind that says, *"Could this person truly be innocent?"* For example:

- **A Missing Witness:** A key witness is absent, and their testimony could have clarified critical facts.
- **Conflicting Testimony:** Two eyewitnesses provide starkly different accounts of the same event.

These are instances where doubt is reasonable and demands careful deliberation.

**Unreasonable Doubt: A Roadblock to Justice**

Unreasonable doubt stems from assumptions, biases, or irrelevant details. For instance:

- **Far-Fetched Theories:** Suggesting a highly improbable scenario without evidence.
- **Prejudices:** Doubts fueled by stereotypes rather than facts.

Courts must balance skepticism with fairness, ensuring doubts are legitimate and not a tactic to derail justice.

**The Thin Line Between Suspicion and Proof**

In criminal trials, suspicion is not enough. Proof is the gold standard, and it must be clear, compelling, and beyond reasonable doubt. Yet, the line between suspicion and proof is often razor-thin and hotly contested.

**Suspicion: The Shadow of Doubt**

Suspicion often arises from circumstantial evidence or gaps in the accused's alibi. For instance:

- **A Suspect's Behavior:** Acting nervous or evasive can raise suspicion but doesn't constitute proof.
- **Proximity to the Crime Scene:** Being nearby doesn't automatically make someone guilty.

**Proof: The Light of Certainty**

Proof converts suspicion into certainty through solid evidence:

- **Forensic Evidence:** Fingerprints or DNA linking the accused to the crime.
- **Direct Witness Testimony:** A credible witness seeing the accused commit the act.

**The Courtroom Dilemma**

Judges and jurors often grapple with this thin line. Is the evidence strong enough to convict, or does it leave room for doubt? This balancing act defines the essence of fair trials.

**Why Doubt Matters**

Doubt is not a weakness of the justice system it's its greatest strength. It forces everyone involved to question, verify, and ensure that the truth is unearthed. But it's also a double-edged sword. Misusing doubt can let the guilty walk free, while ignoring valid doubt can ruin innocent lives.

# Chapter-5

# Practical Application in Real Cases: How the Benefit of Doubt Shapes Justice

# Practical Application in Real Cases: How the Benefit of Doubt Shapes Justice

In the high-stakes world of criminal trials, the benefit of doubt often becomes the tipping point between conviction and acquittal. But how does this principle translate into real-life courtroom drama? How have pivotal cases shaped its application and redefined its role in justice?

This chapter takes you beyond theory, diving into real-world stories where the benefit of doubt wasn't just a legal concept but a lifeline. From high-profile acquittals to cases that sparked national debates, you'll see how justice is influenced by the delicate art of interpreting doubt.

## Case Studies That Redefined the Benefit of Doubt

### 1. The Mystery of Missing Evidence

In a sensational murder trial, the prosecution's case hinged on circumstantial evidence a bloodstain, a witness statement, and a missing weapon. The defense argued that the evidence left too many unanswered questions. The court, recognizing the gaps, acquitted the accused, stating that the benefit of doubt must always favor the accused.

This case highlights a critical lesson: doubt isn't about undermining evidence but about ensuring it's strong enough to justify conviction.

## 2. The Eyewitness Conundrum

An eyewitness identified a man as the culprit in a robbery. But during cross-examination, the defense revealed inconsistencies in the witness's testimony and the possibility of mistaken identity. The court ruled that the evidence was insufficient to convict, setting the accused free.

This landmark case redefined how courts view eyewitness reliability and reinforced the idea that doubt arising from flawed testimony cannot be ignored.

## 3. A Tale of Forensic Failure

In another gripping case, DNA evidence was presented as irrefutable proof of guilt. However, defense experts demonstrated that the forensic analysis was mishandled, leading to contamination. The court recognized the reasonable doubt this created, resulting in an acquittal.

This case underlines the importance of scrutinizing even scientific evidence when doubt arises about its validity.

**Lessons from Acquittals: When Justice Prevailed**

Every acquittal carries a story not just of a person spared from wrongful punishment but of a justice system committed to fairness. What can we learn from these moments when justice truly prevailed?

## 1. The Value of Rigorous Scrutiny

Acquittals often occur because defense lawyers meticulously expose flaws in the prosecution's case. This reinforces the need for courts to examine every shred of evidence critically and without bias.

## 2. The Fragility of Human Testimony

Many acquittals arise from unreliable witnesses. These cases teach us that human memory is fallible, and justice cannot rest solely on statements that may waver under pressure.

## 3. The Role of Modern Technology

Advancements in forensic science have exonerated individuals who were wrongly accused, proving the value of continually questioning and improving investigative methods.

## Why These Cases Matter

These stories aren't just about individuals they're about the system itself. They show how the benefit of doubt prevents the legal system from becoming a conveyor belt of convictions. They inspire confidence that justice, while imperfect, can be compassionate and cautious.

As you delve deeper into this chapter, you'll witness the real impact of doubt on lives, laws, and society. What would you do if you were in the accused's shoes? How would you handle the immense responsibility of deciding guilt or innocence? The answers are waiting in these riveting case studies.

NARAYANASAMY.R

# Chapter-6

# Key Elements That Raise Doubt: The Cracks in the Armor of Conviction

# Key Elements That Raise Doubt: The Cracks in the Armor of Conviction

What makes a seemingly airtight case unravel in a courtroom? What creates those moments when a judge or jury pauses and thinks, *"Is this the whole truth?"* The key lies in the elements that raise doubt flaws in testimony, gaps in evidence, and the enigmatic pull of circumstantial clues. These elements are the fault lines in a case, where the benefit of doubt often emerges as the deciding factor.

This chapter explores the most common triggers of doubt, dissecting how they can turn the tide in a criminal trial. Through compelling examples and real-life scenarios, you'll discover the anatomy of doubt and why it's vital for justice.

**Unreliable Witnesses and Contradictory Testimonies**

**The Fragility of Human Memory**

Witnesses are often the backbone of a case, but human memory is far from perfect. Stress, bias, and the passage of time can distort recollections, making witnesses unreliable even when they are well-intentioned.

For instance, in a high-profile robbery case, a key witness confidently identified the accused. However, during cross-examination, it emerged that the identification took place under poor lighting conditions and with minimal observation time. The court, recognizing the possibility of error, dismissed the testimony as insufficient for conviction.

## The Chaos of Contradictions

What happens when two witnesses describe the same event in completely different ways? Contradictory testimonies can sow seeds of doubt in even the most straightforward cases.

- In one trial, two eyewitnesses gave opposing accounts of a suspect's actions at the crime scene. The discrepancy was so glaring that the court ruled the evidence unreliable, leading to an acquittal.

These instances remind us that justice demands more than confidence it requires consistency and credibility.

## Gaps in Evidence: When Proof Falls Short

### The Missing Link

Sometimes, the prosecution's case appears solid until you notice what isn't there. Missing evidence, unaccounted-for timelines, or unexplored leads can weaken even the most compelling arguments.

- Consider a murder trial where no murder weapon was recovered. Without it, the prosecution's narrative relied heavily on circumstantial evidence, leaving room for doubt about how the crime was committed.

## The Weight of Unanswered Questions

Gaps in evidence don't just raise doubts they create them. If a single piece of crucial evidence is missing, it forces the court to question the completeness of the investigation.

- For example, if forensic results are inconclusive or if surveillance footage mysteriously disappears, it casts a shadow over the integrity of the case.

Such gaps remind us that justice cannot be built on incomplete stories.

## Influence of Circumstantial Evidence

## The Double-Edged Sword

Circumstantial evidence is like a puzzle it connects dots but doesn't always complete the picture. While it can be powerful, it's also prone to interpretation, which opens the door to doubt.

- In a fraud case, the prosecution relied on circumstantial evidence of bank transactions and suspicious emails. However, the defense successfully argued alternative explanations for these actions, introducing doubt that ultimately led to acquittal.

## When Circumstances Mislead

Circumstantial evidence can sometimes point in the wrong direction. Courts are wary of relying too heavily on it without corroboration.

- In a theft case, a suspect was found near the crime scene with no alibi. While this raised suspicion, no direct evidence linked them to the theft. The court concluded that mere presence was insufficient for conviction.

## Why These Elements Matter

Each of these elements unreliable witnesses, gaps in evidence, and circumstantial proof reminds us of the fragility of truth in the courtroom. They challenge the system to dig deeper, question assumptions, and uphold the principle of reasonable doubt.

This chapter invites you to step into the shoes of judges and jurors, grappling with the uncertainties that shape justice. Can you always trust what you see, hear, or think you know? The answers will surprise you, and the stories will stay with you long after you turn the page.

# Chapter-7

# The Role of Cross-Examination: The Battlefield of Truth

# The Role of Cross-Examination: The Battlefield of Truth

In the courtroom, the truth is often buried beneath layers of evidence, emotions, and assumptions. Cross-examination is the sword that cuts through this fog, revealing hidden truths and challenging the narrative presented by the opposing side. It's not just a procedural formality it's the moment where cases are won or lost, where doubts emerge, and where the scales of justice tip.

This chapter explores the art and power of cross-examination. From creating doubt in the minds of jurors to dismantling a seemingly strong case, cross-examination is the ultimate tool in the pursuit of justice.

### How Cross-Examination Can Create Doubt

### Exposing Contradictions

A confident witness can appear invincible until cross-examination begins. A skilled defense lawyer can uncover inconsistencies in their statements, casting doubt on their reliability.

- Imagine a witness who claims to have seen a suspect at a crime scene but, under questioning, admits to poor visibility or prior intoxication. The once-solid testimony now crumbles, leaving the court with more questions than answers.

## Highlighting Bias

Witnesses aren't always impartial. Some may have motives revenge, financial gain, or loyalty that color their testimonies. Cross-examination exposes these hidden agendas.

- In a fraud trial, a key witness admitted under questioning that they had a financial dispute with the accused, casting doubt on their allegations and motives.

## Undermining Expertise

Even expert witnesses aren't immune to scrutiny. Cross-examination tests the foundation of their conclusions, revealing errors or limitations.

- In a medical negligence case, a defense lawyer pointed out flaws in the expert's methodology, leading the jury to question the credibility of their findings.

## Winning Strategies for Defense Lawyers

### 1. The Power of Preparation

Cross-examination is not improvised; it's a carefully orchestrated performance. Defense lawyers study every detail of the case, anticipate answers, and craft questions designed to reveal the truth.

- A lawyer prepared with prior contradictory statements or evidence can corner a witness, exposing discrepancies and weakening the prosecution's case.

## 2. Leading the Witness

The best cross-examinations aren't confrontational they're strategic. By asking closed-ended questions, lawyers guide witnesses into revealing contradictions or admitting uncertainties.

- For example: *"You stated earlier that you saw the accused at 9 PM. Are you certain it wasn't closer to 10 PM?"* Such precision can unravel timelines and challenge credibility.

## 3. The Art of Silence

Sometimes, silence is more powerful than words. After asking a pointed question, a skilled lawyer lets the silence linger, putting pressure on the witness to answer. This often leads to slip-ups or revealing admissions.

## 4. Focus on Key Issues

Effective cross-examination avoids distractions and focuses on critical points that create doubt about the prosecution's case. Every question is deliberate, aimed at building a narrative of uncertainty.

## Cross-Examination in Action: A Game Changer

Real-life cases are full of moments where cross-examination turned the tide:

- **The Case of the Discredited Eyewitness:** A defense lawyer exposed that a witness was 50 meters away in dim lighting, making their identification unreliable. The accused walked free.
- **The Flawed Forensic Report:** By pointing out errors in the collection process during cross-examination, a lawyer invalidated key forensic evidence, leading to acquittal.

These examples show why cross-examination is often referred to as the "trial within a trial."


## Why Cross-Examination Matters

Cross-examination is the cornerstone of adversarial justice. It ensures that witnesses can't simply present unchallenged versions of events and forces every piece of evidence to withstand scrutiny. It's a reminder that doubt is not a flaw in the justice system but its greatest strength a tool to prevent wrongful convictions and uphold fairness.

In this chapter, you'll learn not just how cross-examination works but why it remains one of the most powerful weapons in a lawyer's arsenal. As you turn the pages, prepare to witness the drama, strategy, and sheer brilliance that unfolds when lawyers take the stand to cross-examine.

# Chapter-8

# Landmark Judgments: The Benefit of Doubt in Action

# Landmark Judgments: The Benefit of Doubt in Action

Every courtroom battle leaves behind a legacy a judgment that not only determines the fate of the accused but also shapes the legal landscape for years to come. When it comes to the benefit of doubt, some rulings have gone beyond individual cases to redefine how justice is delivered. These landmark judgments serve as guiding stars, illuminating the principles of fairness, reason, and humanity in criminal law.

This chapter takes you on a journey through iconic Supreme Court and High Court decisions that have transformed the interpretation of the benefit of doubt. Through these cases, you'll witness how the judiciary balances skepticism with evidence, caution with conviction, and the sacred principle of *innocent until proven guilty*.

## Supreme Court Rulings That Changed the Game

### 1. The Golden Rule of Presumption

In *Kali Ram v. State of Himachal Pradesh (1973)*, the Supreme Court emphasized that suspicion, no matter how strong, can never substitute for proof. The judgment reaffirmed the principle that if two views arise from evidence one pointing to guilt and the other to innocence the latter must prevail.

- **Key Takeaway:** This ruling set the gold standard for reasonable doubt, ensuring that courts prioritize fairness over haste in delivering verdicts.

## 2. Strengthening Eyewitness Scrutiny

In *State of Rajasthan v. Bhawani (2003)*, the Supreme Court dealt with the reliability of eyewitness accounts. The Court held that inconsistencies in testimony must be carefully evaluated to determine if they raise reasonable doubt.

- **Key Takeaway:** This case sharpened the judiciary's focus on evaluating human error in testimonies, protecting the innocent from wrongful conviction.

## 3. The DNA Debate

In *Krishna Kumar Malik v. State of Haryana (2011)*, forensic evidence was pivotal, but the Court highlighted the need for corroboration. While scientific evidence is valuable, it cannot singularly override other gaps in proof.

- **Key Takeaway:** The judgment stressed that every element of the prosecution's case must withstand scrutiny, not just its strongest points.

# High Court Decisions That Reshaped Interpretation

## 1. A Conviction Overturned by Doubt

The Bombay High Court's ruling in *Alam Khan v. State of Maharashtra (2015)* dealt with a murder trial where the sole eyewitness was deemed unreliable due to conflicting statements. The Court acquitted the accused, ruling that the benefit of doubt must always favor the accused.

- **Impact:** This case underscored the judiciary's obligation to separate suspicion from certainty.

## 2. Revisiting Circumstantial Evidence

In *Rameshwar Sharma v. State of Uttar Pradesh (2019)*, the Allahabad High Court scrutinized circumstantial evidence in a theft case. The judgment noted that while circumstantial evidence can point to guilt, any missing link in the chain can tilt the scales in favor of acquittal.

- **Impact:** The ruling provided fresh clarity on the role of circumstantial evidence in creating or dispelling reasonable doubt.

## 3. Justice Delayed But Not Denied

The Karnataka High Court's decision in *Suresh Patil v. State of Karnataka (2021)* highlighted the role of benefit of doubt in delayed trials. The Court acquitted an accused in a 20-year-old case, noting that the delay compromised the integrity of evidence.

- **Impact:** This judgment reminded courts of their responsibility to ensure timely justice while safeguarding the rights of the accused.

## Why These Judgments Matter

Each of these rulings demonstrates the judiciary's commitment to fairness and the nuanced application of the benefit of doubt. They illustrate how courts navigate the delicate balance between protecting society and safeguarding individual rights.

These landmark cases aren't just legal precedents they're lessons in humanity. They challenge us to question, reflect, and appreciate the power of doubt as a shield against injustice.

As you explore these judgments, you'll uncover not just the technicalities of the law but the moral compass that guides it. Prepare to be inspired by the judiciary's dedication to upholding the highest ideals of justice, one case at a time.

# Chapter-9

# The Ethical Dilemma: When Doubt Saves the Guilty

# The Ethical Dilemma: When Doubt Saves the Guilty

In the quest for justice, the benefit of doubt is a double-edged sword. It is the cornerstone of fairness, ensuring no innocent person suffers a wrongful conviction. Yet, what happens when this shield inadvertently protects the guilty? This ethical dilemma sits at the heart of criminal law, raising questions that strike at the very core of justice, morality, and societal expectations.

This chapter delves into the tension between law and public sentiment, exploring the profound effects of acquittals on victims, their families, and the broader community. Is it better to risk letting a guilty person walk free than to condemn an innocent one? Or does justice demand a harsher reckoning? The answers lie in the delicate balance courts must maintain.

## Balancing Justice and Public Sentiment

### The Courtroom vs. the Court of Public Opinion

In high-profile cases, public sentiment often runs high, with calls for swift justice and severe punishment. But the judicial system operates on principles, not popularity. Courts must remain impartial, evaluating evidence and applying the law without yielding to the emotional weight of public opinion.

- **Case in Point:** In a controversial acquittal, a court faced backlash for freeing a murder suspect due to lack of evidence. Public outrage was fierce, but the court upheld that doubt however unpopular must benefit the accused.

## The Price of an Acquittal

When the guilty go free, society often perceives it as a failure of justice. However, such outcomes reflect the system's moral commitment to erring on the side of caution. This principle protects everyone, ensuring that the innocent are not collateral damage in the fight against crime.

- **Key Thought:** "Justice is blind, but not deaf to doubt." The judicial process is designed to prioritize fairness over vengeance, even when it challenges societal expectations.

## The Impact on Victims and Their Families

### The Pain of Unanswered Questions

For victims and their families, an acquittal can feel like a betrayal. The emotional toll of seeing a suspect walk free, despite their belief in guilt, can be devastating.

- **Example:** In a landmark sexual assault case, the accused was acquitted due to procedural lapses and conflicting evidence. While the court adhered to legal standards, the victim's family struggled with the perception that justice had not been served.

## A System That Values Truth Over Expediency

The impact on victims is undeniable, but the benefit of doubt exists to ensure justice is not rushed or compromised. Courts are tasked with upholding the principle that punishment must follow proof not merely accusation. This delicate balance often leaves families torn between seeking closure and accepting the complexities of justice.

- **Reflection:** Can a system be called just if it prioritizes the feelings of the aggrieved over the truth? The judiciary's role is to protect the law's integrity, even in the face of human suffering.

**A Necessary Evil or a Moral Imperative?**

The benefit of doubt is not a flaw in the justice system it is its backbone. While it sometimes results in outcomes that society struggles to accept, it ensures that the process remains just, fair, and free from bias.

This chapter invites you to grapple with the ethical questions surrounding doubt. Can justice truly exist without the possibility of error? And how do we reconcile fairness to the accused with the pain it can inflict on victims? These questions are at the heart of the legal system's most profound challenges, and the answers will leave you questioning your own beliefs about justice and morality.

# Chapter-10

# Safeguarding the Innocent: The Way Forward

## Safeguarding the Innocent: The Way Forward

In the labyrinth of justice, the ultimate goal is to protect the innocent while ensuring the guilty face their due. Yet, the justice system is not infallible errors in investigations, weak prosecutions, and systemic gaps can cast long shadows over fairness. This chapter charts a way forward, exploring strategies to enhance the integrity of criminal trials while honoring the principle of *innocent until proven guilty*.

From adopting cutting-edge investigative techniques to building airtight prosecution cases, the future of justice lies in refining the process rather than compromising on its ideals.

### Enhancing Investigation Techniques

### 1. The Science of Precision: Leveraging Forensic Technology

Modern crimes demand modern solutions. Forensic advancements such as DNA analysis, digital forensics, and AI-driven evidence mapping can significantly reduce errors in investigations. These technologies provide objective insights, minimizing reliance on subjective testimony.

- **Example:** DNA evidence exonerated a man wrongfully accused of assault after nearly two decades in prison, proving the transformative power of precise investigations.

## 2. Training Law Enforcement: Bridging the Knowledge Gap

Even the most advanced tools are ineffective without skilled personnel. Regular training for law enforcement on evidence collection, preservation, and interrogation techniques is crucial.

- **Key Takeaway:** A well-trained officer is the first line of defense against wrongful convictions and the misuse of evidence.

## 3. Independent Oversight Mechanisms

To prevent bias or procedural lapses, investigative agencies should operate under independent oversight. Such mechanisms can ensure accountability and maintain public trust.

- **Reflection:** Can we create a justice system that is both efficient and immune to external pressures? Oversight might just be the answer.

## Building Stronger Prosecution Cases

## 1. Comprehensive Evidence Gathering

Prosecutors must move beyond circumstantial evidence to build cases rooted in concrete proof. Every link in the chain of evidence must be robust, leaving no room for doubt.

- **Example:** In a landmark judgment, the Supreme Court criticized the prosecution for relying solely on a coerced confession, underscoring the need for corroborative evidence.

## 2. Collaboration Between Police and Prosecutors

Effective prosecution begins with seamless coordination between investigators and legal teams. Early involvement of prosecutors in investigations can help shape cases with a focus on legal requirements and trial readiness.

- **Insight:** A collaborative approach ensures that cases are built on a foundation of legal strategy rather than reactive measures.

## 3. Strengthening Witness Protection Programs

Witnesses are the backbone of many criminal cases, but fear and intimidation often silence them. A robust witness protection mechanism is essential to encourage honest testimony.

- **Case in Point:** A key witness in a high-profile case recanted their statement after threats, leading to the collapse of the prosecution's case. A secure and supportive system could have prevented this outcome.

## Reimagining Justice: A Unified Approach

Safeguarding the innocent doesn't require reinventing the wheel it demands refining and reinforcing existing systems. By enhancing investigative rigor and building stronger prosecution cases, we can ensure that the justice system fulfills its true purpose: protecting the innocent while delivering accountability for the guilty.

As you journey through this chapter, you'll discover that the way forward isn't just about technology or law it's about commitment. Commitment to fairness, truth, and the unwavering pursuit of justice. Together, these elements form the blueprint for a future where the innocent can sleep soundly, knowing the system stands firmly on their side.

# Chapter-11

# The Global Perspective: The Benefit of Doubt Across Borders

# The Global Perspective: The Benefit of Doubt Across Borders

Justice knows no boundaries, yet the principles that guide it can vary dramatically from one legal system to another. While the *benefit of doubt* is a core tenet of criminal law worldwide, how it is applied can differ based on cultural values, historical contexts, and legal frameworks. In this chapter, we embark on a global journey, comparing how the *benefit of doubt* plays out in different legal systems and what India can learn from the practices of other nations.

By delving into both the commonalities and unique approaches across borders, we will uncover new insights into how justice is balanced in different parts of the world, enriching our understanding of the universal need for fairness and due process.

**The Benefit of Doubt in Other Legal Systems**

**1. The Common Law Tradition: Protecting the Innocent at All Costs**

In countries with a common law system, like the United States and the United Kingdom, the *benefit of doubt* is fundamental to ensuring that the presumption of innocence is upheld. The *beyond a reasonable doubt* standard is a cornerstone of these systems, where the prosecution must prove guilt with irrefutable evidence.

- **Example:** In *R v. Dudley and Stephens (1884)*, the English court acquitted two sailors charged with murder after they had killed a fellow crew member for survival. Despite their guilt, the court ruled that the benefit of doubt should apply in extreme circumstances.

## 2. Civil Law Systems: A Structured Approach to Doubt

In civil law countries like France and Germany, the *benefit of doubt* is more rigidly defined within the written code. Judges play a more active role in investigating the facts, leaving less room for uncertainty in legal outcomes. However, the principle of *doubt* still guides their verdicts, often used to avoid wrongful convictions.

- **Key Takeaway:** In civil law countries, while judges are more investigative, they still prioritize doubt as a safeguard against injustice, although the process differs from the adversarial model seen in common law jurisdictions.

## 3. Restorative Justice in Indigenous Legal Systems

In some indigenous legal systems, doubt is viewed not just as a legal tool but as a cultural one. Many indigenous communities focus on healing and reconciliation rather than retribution, providing a unique perspective on the *benefit of doubt* as a means to restore balance and peace within the community.

- **Reflection:** These alternative systems remind us that the *benefit of doubt* is not only a legal tool but also a cultural and philosophical choice about how societies view wrongdoing and repair.

## Comparative Analysis: Indian vs. International Law

### 1. The Indian Approach: Preserving the Sanctity of Doubt

India, rooted in its colonial past, inherited the British legal system. The *benefit of doubt* plays a critical role in Indian criminal law, enshrined in the presumption of innocence under Article 21 of the Constitution. However, courts in India sometimes face pressures that influence the application of this principle. Public opinion, political climate, and socio-economic factors often make the application of doubt complex.

- **Key Example:** In *State of Rajasthan v. Kashi Ram (2006)*, the Supreme Court reiterated that doubt must always benefit the accused, even in the face of societal pressure for harsher penalties.

### 2. Lessons from the United States: High Stakes of Doubt

The U.S. system places a high emphasis on *reasonable doubt*, with the landmark case *In re Winship (1970)* solidifying the requirement that a criminal conviction cannot stand unless the evidence leaves no room for reasonable doubt. While this maxim helps protect the innocent, it has also sparked debates about its application, especially in cases involving racial or socio-economic factors.

- **Insight:** While India and the U.S. share a common law heritage, the U.S. legal system places greater emphasis on procedural safeguards, which could serve as valuable lessons for Indian law.

## 3. The French Approach: A Different Balance of Doubt

French criminal law, based on civil law principles, differs significantly from India's. The judiciary in France is more inquisitorial, meaning judges themselves investigate the facts of the case. While *doubt* is still a guiding principle, the role of the judge means there is less reliance on the parties to raise reasonable doubt.

- **Key Takeaway:** In France, the idea of doubt is tied to the judge's duty to investigate thoroughly, highlighting the potential benefits of a more active judicial role in uncovering truth, something India could learn from in high-profile cases.

## 4. Comparative Verdicts: What Can India Learn?

While the core principle of the *benefit of doubt* remains largely the same across borders, the application can differ significantly. India's judicial system, with its heavy caseload and slow process, sometimes struggles to ensure that reasonable doubt is fully explored in every case. Lessons from international systems could lead to reforms that ensure a more thorough examination of evidence and a quicker, more transparent trial process.

- **Insight:** India may benefit from adopting more proactive investigative methods or integrating restorative justice principles in certain cases, creating a more holistic approach to justice.

## A World of Doubt: Embracing Global Insights

The *benefit of doubt* is not confined to one country or one legal system it is a universal principle of justice. By examining how different nations interpret and apply this concept, we gain a deeper understanding of its complexity and its essential role in safeguarding the rights of the accused.

This chapter pushes the boundaries of traditional legal analysis, encouraging readers to consider how India's legal system can evolve by borrowing from global best practices. Through this comparative lens, you will see the true power of doubt not as a flaw in the system, but as a necessary force to ensure fairness, truth, and justice for all.

# Chapter-12

# Criticism and Controversy: The Shadows of Doubt

# Criticism and Controversy: The Shadows of Doubt

The *benefit of doubt* is a cornerstone of justice, but like any principle, it is not without its critics. In this chapter, we delve into the ongoing debates surrounding this vital legal concept. Is it too lenient? Does it unintentionally protect the guilty? The application of doubt, though essential for preserving fairness, can stir emotions and spark controversy, especially when the stakes are high.

As we explore these criticisms, we'll examine both sides of the argument and challenge the very foundations of this principle asking whether it's truly a safeguard for the innocent or a potential loophole for the guilty. Get ready for a thought-provoking exploration of the dark side of doubt.

### Is the Principle Too Lenient?

### 1. The Fine Line Between Caution and Over-Caution

The *benefit of doubt* is meant to prevent wrongful convictions, but in some cases, it has been criticized for making the legal system too lenient. Advocates argue that in high-profile cases, where public sentiment demands justice, the constant plea for doubt can lead to acquittals that seem unjust. Is it possible that the principle, in its pursuit of fairness, sometimes lets the guilty walk free?

- **Example:** In certain cases of violent crime, where overwhelming evidence points toward guilt but not beyond *all* reasonable doubt, the accused may be acquitted, leaving victims and their families devastated.

## 2. The Burden of Proof: A Double-Edged Sword

While the presumption of innocence protects the accused, it also places a heavy burden on the prosecution. In some cases, even if the evidence points strongly toward guilt, if there is any reasonable doubt, the accused must be acquitted. Critics argue this places an undue burden on the victims and their families, leaving them without justice.

- **Insight:** How much doubt is "reasonable"? The answer is often subjective, leading to potential misapplications of justice that seem lenient at the expense of the greater good.

## 3. Legal Loopholes: Exploiting the Benefit of Doubt

Some argue that the *benefit of doubt* can be exploited by clever defense lawyers, using every technicality to cast doubt on the evidence, regardless of its strength. These tactics, while within the letter of the law, may seem unjust to the public when they result in the acquittal of the guilty.

- **Case Study:** High-profile defense attorneys often argue that *suspicion* or *lack of clarity* is enough to create reasonable doubt, even if the evidence strongly suggests guilt. This manipulation of the system is seen by critics as an abuse of the principle.

## Debate: Does the Benefit of Doubt Encourage Criminals?

### 1. Shield for the Guilty?

One of the most potent criticisms of the *benefit of doubt* is that it may serve as a shield for criminals, especially in cases with circumstantial evidence. If the evidence is not airtight, even if the facts point toward a likely crime, the accused may walk free. Could this lead to a culture where criminals feel emboldened, knowing that a single shred of doubt can set them free?

- **Example:** In cases where the accused is a repeat offender, but the evidence isn't overwhelming, the *benefit of doubt* may allow them to evade justice once again. Does this not create a system where the guilty can slip through the cracks?

### 2. The Ripple Effect on Society

When a guilty person is acquitted, it's not just the victim who suffers society at large feels the impact. Critics argue that the *benefit of doubt*, when misapplied, erodes public trust in the justice system. If people perceive that criminals are not being held accountable, it undermines faith in the law itself, leading to social unrest.

- **Reflection:** When a case is widely seen as a miscarriage of justice, the result is not just a legal defeat it can stir public outrage, making it seem like the system is failing to protect society.

## 3. Can the Justice System Afford to Be This Cautious?

With the rise of high-profile criminal cases and media scrutiny, the legal system's caution in applying the *benefit of doubt* can come into question. Critics argue that, in an age where information is abundant and public opinion is strong, the principle may be too cautious, allowing criminals to escape while justice is delayed for victims.

- **Key Insight:** Some believe the scale has tipped too far in favor of the accused, leading to a situation where protecting the rights of the accused might outweigh the need for swift justice for the victims.

### A Necessary Debate

While the *benefit of doubt* is an essential element of any fair and just legal system, these criticisms highlight the tension between fairness and accountability. The question remains: how much doubt is *reasonable*? Is there a tipping point where the protection of the accused comes at the cost of justice for the victim and society?

In this chapter, we've explored the challenging balance between leniency and justice, and while the answers may not be clear-cut, the debate is essential. As we move forward in the book, the question remains: is doubt a safeguard of justice, or has it become a loophole for the guilty? Only time and continued reflection will tell.

# Chapter-13

# The Lawyer's Toolkit: Arguing for the Benefit of Doubt

# The Lawyer's Toolkit: Arguing for the Benefit of Doubt

In the complex landscape of criminal defense, *the benefit of doubt* is both a powerful tool and a delicate balancing act. For a defense lawyer, it's not just a concept it's a strategy that can make the difference between conviction and acquittal. But how do lawyers use the *benefit of doubt* effectively to craft their defense? What key questions must be asked to ensure that doubt is properly introduced and amplified in the minds of the judge or jury?

This chapter dives deep into the lawyer's toolkit, equipping you with the essential strategies, techniques, and mindset required to argue for the benefit of doubt in the courtroom. If you've ever wondered what separates the average advocate from the exceptional one, the answer lies in how they present doubt as a compelling, irrefutable force of justice.

**Crafting a Defense Strategy: Mastering the Art of Doubt**

**1. Starting with the Presumption of Innocence**

Every defense begins with a simple, yet profound truth: *the accused is innocent until proven guilty*. Embrace this presumption and make it your foundation. As a defense lawyer, it's your job to highlight and emphasize this cornerstone principle. Your strategy should always center around the idea that the prosecution has failed to prove guilt beyond a reasonable doubt.

- **Action Tip:** Begin your argument by reminding the court of the sacredness of the presumption of innocence. This sets the tone for your case, reinforcing that the burden of proof lies solely with the prosecution.

## 2. Creating Holes in the Prosecution's Case

To create doubt, you need to methodically attack the prosecution's evidence. Highlight inconsistencies, unreliable testimonies, and weaknesses in the chain of evidence. The smallest crack in the prosecution's case can be the opening you need to cast a shadow of doubt.

- **Example:** *In a murder trial, a defense lawyer noticed discrepancies in the timeline of the victim's last known moments. The prosecution's alibi fell apart, planting seeds of doubt in the jury's mind.*
- **Action Tip:** Prepare by dissecting every piece of evidence presented by the prosecution. Your goal is to challenge its credibility, relevance, and weight.

## 3. Shifting the Burden of Proof

Argue that the prosecution has failed to meet the highest standard of proof: *beyond a reasonable doubt*. Point out that if there is even the smallest lingering doubt in the evidence, the case cannot be proven.

- **Action Tip:** Remind the court that reasonable doubt is not just an abstract idea it's a tangible standard that demands full, irrefutable proof. Even a small doubt in the evidence is enough to tip the scale toward acquittal.

## 4. Exploiting Contradictions and Inconsistencies

One of the best ways to introduce doubt is by emphasizing contradictions in witness statements or evidence. Inconsistencies in the case narrative create space for doubt, making the prosecution's version of events harder to believe.

- **Example:** *A witness in a robbery case gave multiple versions of the event in earlier testimonies. The defense lawyer used these contradictions to argue that the witness was unreliable, casting doubt on the entire case.*
- **Action Tip:** Create a visual timeline or diagram showing conflicting testimonies, helping the judge or jury visualize the flaws in the prosecution's case.

### Key Questions Every Advocate Must Ask

When preparing to argue for the *benefit of doubt*, the most important question a defense lawyer can ask is: *How can I cast doubt on the prosecution's evidence, witnesses, and narrative?* Below are the key questions that should guide every advocate's strategy in building a compelling case for doubt:

### 1. Is the Evidence Sufficient to Prove Guilt Beyond a Reasonable Doubt?

This is the foundation of your entire argument. Examine every detail of the evidence presented by the prosecution. Is there a piece of critical evidence missing? Is the evidence circumstantial, or does it fail to directly link the accused to the crime?

- **Insight:** A strong defense hinges on pointing out that the evidence falls short of the *beyond a reasonable doubt* standard.

## 2. Are the Witnesses Credible?

Every witness must be scrutinized. Are there any credibility issues, such as prior inconsistent statements, bias, or motives to lie?

- **Action Tip:** Challenge the reliability of witnesses by pointing out past discrepancies or suggesting potential biases that may have influenced their testimonies.

## 3. Is There Any Alternative Explanation for the Events?

One effective way to introduce doubt is by offering an alternative explanation that fits the evidence. Does the evidence leave room for another interpretation of the facts?

- **Example:** In a theft case, could the accused have been in the area by coincidence, or could someone else have committed the crime while the accused was unaware?
- **Action Tip:** Present a plausible alternative scenario that casts doubt on the prosecution's case without directly accusing others.

## 4. Was the Investigation Thorough and Unbiased?

Was the investigation conducted fairly and thoroughly, or were key pieces of evidence ignored or mishandled? If the investigation was flawed, the *benefit of doubt* naturally tilts in favor of the accused.

- **Key Takeaway:** In some cases, pointing out investigative oversights, such as missing evidence or rushed conclusions, can be the key to undermining the prosecution's case.

## 5. What Are the Emotional and Psychological Impacts on the Jury or Judge?

Doubt isn't always logical it's psychological too. Are there any emotional appeals in the case that might cloud judgment?

- **Action Tip:** Carefully observe the emotional atmosphere in the courtroom and use it to your advantage by injecting rational arguments when tensions are high.

**The Final Word: Empowering the Defense Lawyer**

In this section, we've uncovered not just the tools, but the mindset needed to argue for the *benefit of doubt*. From crafting a defense strategy to asking the right questions, every lawyer should approach each case with the aim of amplifying doubt, shining a light on weaknesses, and ensuring that justice is served. This chapter equips you with the knowledge to stand firm, challenge the prosecution, and defend your client with skill and confidence.

The power of doubt lies in its ability to dismantle certainty, and when used effectively, it can become an advocate's most potent weapon.

# Chapter-14

# Conclusion: A Pillar of Justice and Humanity

## Conclusion: A Pillar of Justice and Humanity

As we reach the final chapter of this exploration, we pause to reflect on the immense power and profound significance of the *benefit of doubt* in criminal law. More than just a legal principle, it serves as a cornerstone of justice, ensuring that fairness and humanity remain at the heart of every trial.

The *benefit of doubt* is a shield against the imperfections of the justice system, acting as a safeguard to protect the innocent and uphold the integrity of law. It stands as a reminder that the scales of justice must always tip in favor of protecting human dignity, even when the evidence is not conclusive. This principle safeguards against wrongful convictions and preserves the very essence of justice. It is a shield that defends both the individual and the society from the consequences of a rushed or mistaken judgment.

But why does the *benefit of doubt* remain so crucial? Why does it continue to serve as a pillar of justice, not only in India but across the world? The answer lies in its timeless relevance, its capacity to adapt to the evolving complexities of law, and its role in balancing the scales of justice with wisdom and compassion.

### The Everlasting Relevance of the Benefit of Doubt

In an ever-changing world, the *benefit of doubt* remains an unshakable foundation of the criminal justice system. As societies evolve, as new forms of evidence emerge, and as laws adapt to modern challenges, the need for this principle remains constant. In fact, it is more relevant today than ever before.

## 1. A Safeguard in an Imperfect System

Every legal system is imperfect. No system is infallible, and mistakes are inevitable. This is where the *benefit of doubt* plays its most vital role. It acknowledges that human error whether in investigation, evidence handling, or even in interpreting the law is part of the process. The principle ensures that these errors don't come at the cost of someone's liberty, reputation, or life.

The *benefit of doubt* also acts as a constant reminder that the judicial system must never lean too heavily on suspicion or assumption. It forces the system to demand that the evidence, the truth, and the facts be beyond all doubt before anyone's life is irrevocably altered.

## 2. The Power to Protect the Innocent

In every courtroom, behind the legalese and technical arguments, is a person's life at stake. The *benefit of doubt* is not just a tool for lawyers it's a protection for every individual. When a jury or judge applies the *benefit of doubt*, they are protecting more than just the legal rights of the accused. They are protecting the very core of justice and human rights, ensuring that no one is unjustly condemned based on unreliable or insufficient evidence.

## 3. A Moral Compass in Law

The *benefit of doubt* serves as a moral compass for the legal profession. It helps attorneys, judges, and jurors look beyond the rhetoric and emotions that may cloud their judgment and focus on the higher moral obligation to seek truth and justice. It helps ensure that the judicial system does not become a mechanism for oppression, but instead remains a force for good, upholding the sanctity of human life and dignity.

## 4. Shaping the Future of Justice

As we look to the future, the relevance of the *benefit of doubt* will continue to resonate across the evolving landscape of criminal law. With advancements in forensic science, digital evidence, and new legal interpretations, the principle will guide how justice systems adapt to meet new challenges. It will shape how we view fairness, equality, and due process in the years to come.

In the end, the *benefit of doubt* is not just a legal safeguard it is a profound commitment to humanity itself. It reminds us that in the pursuit of justice, we must never forget the preciousness of human life and the irreversibility of decisions that can alter it. Its everlasting relevance lies not only in its ability to protect the innocent but also in its power to guide us toward a more just and humane society.

## A Call for Reflection and Action

As we conclude, we encourage you whether a legal professional, a student, or a curious reader to reflect on the weight of the *benefit of doubt* in our legal systems. This principle shapes the very core of how we define justice, fairness, and humanity. In every case, it is a call for scrutiny, for compassion, and for reason.

Ultimately, the *benefit of doubt* is not a mere abstract concept it is a powerful, living force that governs how we judge, how we decide, and how we act in the face of uncertainty. Understanding its significance can help us navigate not just the world of law, but also the world of human interactions, where doubt and certainty often coexist. The *benefit of doubt* is more than just a legal tool; it is a moral imperative a reminder that justice must always be tempered with compassion and wisdom.

NARAYANASAMY.R

# Chapter-15

# Annexures

# Annexures

As we conclude this deep dive into the *benefit of doubt*, this section serves as a crucial resource to enhance your understanding and help you navigate the complex legal landscape. Here, we provide an invaluable collection of materials that complement the key themes explored throughout the book. These annexures are designed to offer clarity, reinforce learning, and give you the tools to apply these concepts in real-world legal practice. Whether you're a student, practitioner, or legal enthusiast, these annexures will become your go-to reference for building a solid foundation in criminal law.

---

**Glossary of Legal Terms**

In the world of law, terminology can often be overwhelming, filled with Latin phrases and complex legal jargon. To demystify these terms and make them more accessible, this glossary serves as your quick guide to understanding the key words and concepts you'll encounter throughout this book. From *beyond a reasonable doubt* to *circumstantial evidence*, each term is explained in simple language, making it easier to grasp their significance within the context of the *benefit of doubt* principle.

**Example Terms:**

- **Beyond a Reasonable Doubt**: The highest standard of proof in a criminal trial, which demands that there be no other logical explanation for the evidence presented except the accused's guilt.

- **Presumption of Innocence**: A foundational legal principle that ensures that a accused is considered innocent until proven guilty in a court of law.
- **Circumstantial Evidence**: Evidence that suggests a fact but does not directly prove it, often used to infer the existence of certain elements in a case.
- **Burden of Proof**: The responsibility placed on the prosecution to prove the guilt of the accused, which must be done beyond a reasonable doubt.

By the end of this glossary, you'll feel more confident in navigating the language of the courtroom and applying these terms with ease.

## Landmark Case Summaries

In this section, we revisit some of the most pivotal rulings in legal history that have shaped the application of the *benefit of doubt*. These landmark decisions are not just case studies; they are the foundation upon which our understanding of justice is built. Each case summary highlights how the principle of *reasonable doubt* was interpreted, how it influenced the outcome of the case, and what lasting impact it had on future legal proceedings.

### Notable Cases Include:

### 1. Kali Ram v. State of Himachal Pradesh (1973 AIR 2773)

**Background:**
In this case, the accused was charged with the murder of his wife. The prosecution relied heavily on circumstantial evidence.

## Judgment:

The Supreme Court emphasized the principle of *benefit of doubt*, stating:

- If two views are possible one pointing to the guilt of the accused and the other to their innocence the benefit of doubt should go to the accused.
- Conviction cannot be based on suspicion or probabilities but must rest on concrete proof.

## Significance:

The case established that in the absence of reliable evidence, the accused must be acquitted.

## 2. Sharad Birdhichand Sarda v. State of Maharashtra (1984 AIR 1622)

### Background:

This case involved the death of a woman, and the accused husband was charged with abetment to suicide and cruelty.

### Judgment:

The Supreme Court laid down the famous *five golden principles* for proving a case based on circumstantial evidence, often referred to as the *panchsheel of evidence*:

1. The circumstances must be fully established.
2. The circumstances must unerringly point to the guilt of the accused.
3. The circumstances should exclude every possible hypothesis except the one that establishes guilt.

4. There must be a clear link between the chain of circumstances.
5. The chain of evidence must lead to only one conclusion the guilt of the accused.

**Significance:**
The Court acquitted the accused by applying the *benefit of doubt* due to gaps in the evidence chain.

## 3. State of U.P. v. Krishna Gopal and Another (1988 AIR 2154)

**Background:**
The accused were charged with murder during a communal riot. The trial court acquitted them, but the High Court convicted them based on eyewitness accounts.

**Judgment:**
The Supreme Court held that in criminal cases, the prosecution must prove the case beyond a reasonable doubt.

- The principle of *benefit of doubt* protects the accused if the evidence is insufficient or contradictory.
- It ensures that innocent individuals are not convicted due to weak or incomplete evidence.

**Significance:**
This case reinforced the idea that suspicion, no matter how strong, cannot replace proof.

## 4. Bhim Singh v. State of Haryana (2002 AIR 437)

### Background:
The accused were convicted of murder based on circumstantial evidence and alleged eyewitness accounts.

### Judgment:
The Supreme Court reiterated:

- If the prosecution fails to prove its case conclusively, the accused must be given the *benefit of doubt*.
- Eyewitness accounts must be scrutinized critically, especially if they seem unreliable.

### Significance:
The Court acquitted the accused, highlighting that justice errs on the side of caution to prevent the wrongful conviction of innocents.


## 5. Narendra Singh v. State of M.P. (2004 AIR 26)

### Background:
The case involved charges of murder, where the accused's involvement was questioned due to contradictory evidence.

### Judgment:
The Court held:

- The prosecution must establish its case beyond reasonable doubt, and any lacuna in evidence entitles the accused to acquittal.

- Circumstantial evidence must be consistent and conclusive.

**Significance:**
The Court emphasized that any reasonable doubt in the prosecution's case should lead to an acquittal to uphold the principle of fairness.

These cases underscore the importance of the *benefit of doubt* principle in ensuring justice and protecting individuals from wrongful convictions. Let me know if you'd like more details on any specific case or their application in the Indian legal system!

## Legal Provisions and References

Understanding the legal framework surrounding the *benefit of doubt* is essential for anyone navigating the criminal justice system. In this section, we provide direct references to the relevant sections of Indian law, international legal instruments, and statutes that relate to the concept of *reasonable doubt*, presumption of innocence, and the rules of evidence.

### Key Provisions Include:

- **Indian Penal Code (IPC), Sections 101–104**: These sections outline the general principles of criminal liability, including the role of evidence, and how doubt plays a crucial role in establishing guilt.

- **Criminal Procedure Code (CrPC), Section 232**: This section deals with the *discharge* of a case, emphasizing how a judge may discharge the accused if the evidence presented does not suffice to prove guilt beyond a reasonable doubt.
- **Indian Evidence Act, Section 3**: Defines what constitutes "evidence" in a trial and the role of circumstantial evidence in shaping the verdict, providing the foundation for the benefit of doubt in evidence analysis.
- **International Covenant on Civil and Political Rights (ICCPR), Article 14**: A global reference, this provision outlines the basic principles of fair trial, including the presumption of innocence, a cornerstone in ensuring that *doubt* plays its necessary role in global justice systems.

These legal provisions not only strengthen your understanding of the book's core concepts but also provide practical tools for applying them in legal practice.

## Final Thoughts

These annexures are more than just a collection of resources they are the keys to unlocking a deeper understanding of the *benefit of doubt* and its role in the criminal justice system. By combining essential legal definitions, landmark cases, and statutory references, we've crafted a comprehensive toolkit that will serve you long after you've finished this book. Whether you're looking to revisit a complex concept, reference a case, or explore the legal provisions in more detail, these annexures are designed to support your ongoing journey in the world of law.

With these resources at your fingertips, you'll be better equipped to navigate the intricacies of the legal system and confidently apply the *benefit of doubt* in your own practice or studies.

www.ingramcontent.com/pod-product-compliance
Lightning Source LLC
Chambersburg PA
CBHW070349230526
45471CB00006B/2479

# GI Meds Made Easy

Callie Parker

Copyright © 2025 by Callie Parker

All rights reserved.

No portion of this book may be reproduced in any form without written permission from the publisher or author, except as permitted by U.S. copyright law.

🎉 **Wait!** Before You Dive In... Grab Your FREE Nursing Study Survival Kit!

Nursing school is no joke—that's why MadeEasy.Academy is committed to sending the ladder back down and rescuing those of you in the trenches!

Ready to study smarter, not harder? We've got exactly what you need.

Your FREE NCLEX in My Sleep Bundle Includes:

☑ Who's Dying First? The Prioritization Playbook: Because patient safety is kind of a big deal. 😬
☑ Flashcard Frenzy: Memorize or Die Trying: Pre-made Anki cards to save your sanity.
☑ WTF Does This Lab Value Mean? Cheat Sheet: No more second-guessing normal vs. "oh sh*t" levels.
☑ NCLEX Mnemonics That Stick (Like Tape on an IV Line): Memory hacks you'll actually remember.
☑ Med Math Without the Mental Breakdown: Because no one wants to commit a dosage error. 😬

Head over to MadeEasy.Academy to grab your bundle. Let's turn nursing school stress into success!

# But that's not all...

# 🎁 BONUS 🎁

## Your Bundle Includes an Exclusive 50% OFF Discount Code for your next course at Made Easy Academy
(Launching June 1!)

At [MadeEasy.Academy](MadeEasy.Academy) we don't just simplify nursing—we transform it into an effortless, memorable study process.

For each topic, you'll follow our step by step success guide:

 **Step 1. Grab your cheat sheet:** All key points, zero fluff.

 **Step 2. Read your mnemonic poem:** Clever rhymes to make information stick.

 **Step 3. Take your fill-in-the-blank quiz:** Test your recall without the overwhelm.

 **Step 4. Complete your NCLEX challenge:** Realistic practice questions with clear rationales.

 **Step 5. Walk Into the NCLEX Like a Boss:** Confident, prepared, and ready to pass.

Right now, we're laser-focused on Pharmacology, but we'll soon expand into other crucial nursing topics! Have a topic you want us to cover next? Shoot us an email at hello@madeeasy.academy—we've got you!

# Contents

| | |
|---|---|
| Chapter | 1 |
| Pharmacology Mind Maps | 6 |
| Pharmacology Mnemonics | 8 |
| Medication Mind Map Template | 10 |
| 1. Adalimumab (Humira) | 11 |
| 2. Albendazole (Albenza) | 13 |
| 3. Alosetron (Lotronex) | 15 |
| 4. Alpha-Galactosidase (Beano) | 17 |
| 5. Aluminum Hydroxide/Magnesium Hydroxide (Maalox, Mylanta) | 19 |
| 6. Alvimopan (Entereg) | 21 |
| 7. Aprepitant (Emend) | 23 |
| 8. Atropine (Atropine Ophthalmic) | 25 |
| 9. Azathioprine (Imuran) | 27 |
| 10. Barium Sulfate Suspension | 29 |
| 11. Bifidobacterium Infantis (Align) | 31 |
| 12. Bisacodyl (Dulcolax) | 33 |
| 13. Bismuth Subsalicylate (Pepto-Bismol, Kaopectate) | 35 |
| 14. Budesonide (Entocort EC, Uceris) | 37 |
| 15. Calcium Carbonate (Tums) | 39 |

| | | |
|---|---|---|
| 16. | Castor Oil | 41 |
| 17. | Cholestyramine (Questran) | 43 |
| 18. | Cimetidine (Tagamet) | 45 |
| 19. | Ciprofloxacin (Cipro) | 47 |
| 20. | Colesevelam (Welchol) | 49 |
| 21. | Dexlansoprazole (Dexilant) | 51 |
| 22. | Dicyclomine (Bentyl) | 53 |
| 23. | Dimenhydrinate (Dramamine) | 55 |
| 24. | Diphenoxylate/Atropine (Lomotil) | 57 |
| 25. | Docusate Sodium (Colace) | 59 |
| 26. | Eluxadoline (Viberzi) | 61 |
| 27. | Erythromycin (Erythrocin) | 63 |
| 28. | Esomeprazole (Nexium) | 65 |
| 29. | Famotidine (Pepcid) | 67 |
| 30. | Ferrous Sulfate (Iron) | 69 |
| 31. | Fidaxomicin (Dificid) | 71 |
| 32. | Glycerin Suppositories | 73 |
| 33. | Glycopyrrolate (Robinul) | 75 |
| 34. | Golimumab (Simponi) | 77 |
| 35. | Hydrocortisone Rectal Foam (Cortifoam) | 79 |
| 36. | Hydrocortisone Suppositories/Cream (Anusol-HC) | 81 |
| 37. | Hyoscyamine (Levsin) | 83 |
| 38. | Infliximab (Remicade) | 85 |
| 39. | Ivermectin (Stromectol) | 87 |
| 40. | Lactobacillus Acidophilus | 89 |
| 41. | Lactulose (Constulose, Generlac) | 91 |
| 42. | Lansoprazole (Prevacid) | 93 |
| 43. | Ledipasvir/Sofosbuvir (Harvoni) | 95 |

| | | |
|---|---|---|
| 44. | Linaclotide (Linzess) | 97 |
| 45. | Liraglutide (Saxenda) | 99 |
| 46. | Loperamide (Imodium) | 101 |
| 47. | Lubiprostone (Amitiza) | 103 |
| 48. | Magnesium Citrate | 105 |
| 49. | Magnesium Hydroxide (Milk of Magnesia) | 107 |
| 50. | Mebendazole (Emverm) | 109 |
| 51. | Mesalamine (Asacol, Pentasa, Lialda) | 111 |
| 52. | Mesalamine Rectal (Canasa, Rowasa) | 113 |
| 53. | Metoclopramide (Reglan) | 115 |
| 54. | Metronidazole (Flagyl) | 117 |
| 55. | Misoprostol (Cytotec) | 119 |
| 56. | Neomycin | 121 |
| 57. | Nitroglycerin Rectal (Rectiv) | 123 |
| 58. | Nizatidine (Axid) | 125 |
| 59. | Obeticholic Acid (Ocaliva) | 127 |
| 60. | Omeprazole (Prilosec) | 129 |
| 61. | Ondansetron (Zofran) | 131 |
| 62. | Orlistat (Xenical, Alli) | 133 |
| 63. | Pancrelipase (Creon, Zenpep, Pancrease) | 135 |
| 64. | Pantoprazole (Protonix) | 137 |
| 65. | Peppermint Oil Capsules (IBgard) | 139 |
| 66. | Phenylephrine Rectal (Preparation H) | 141 |
| 67. | Plecanatide (Trulance) | 143 |
| 68. | Polyethylene Glycol (MiraLAX) | 145 |
| 69. | Prochlorperazine (Compazine) | 147 |
| 70. | Promethazine (Phenergan) | 149 |
| 71. | Prucalopride (Motegrity) | 151 |

72. Psyllium Fiber (Metamucil) — 153
73. Rifaximin (Xifaxan) — 155
74. Saccharomyces boulardii (Florastor) — 157
75. Scopolamine Patch (Transderm-Scop) — 159
76. Semaglutide (Wegovy) — 161
77. Senna (Senokot, Ex-Lax) — 163
78. Sennosides/Docusate (Senna-S) — 165
79. Simethicone (Gas-X, Mylicon) — 167
80. Sodium Bicarbonate (Alka-Seltzer) — 169
81. Sodium Phosphate Enema (Fleet Enema) — 171
82. Sofosbuvir (Sovaldi) — 173
83. Sucralfate (Carafate) — 175
84. Sulfasalazine (Azulfidine) — 177
85. Teduglutide (Gattex) — 179
86. Tegaserod (Zelnorm) — 181
87. Tenofovir (Viread) — 183
88. Ursodiol (Actigall, Urso Forte) — 185
89. Ustekinumab (Stelara) — 187
90. Vancomycin Oral (Vancocin) — 189
91. Vedolizumab (Entyvio) — 191
92. Vitamin B12 (Cyanocobalamin) — 193

# WHY Made Easy Works

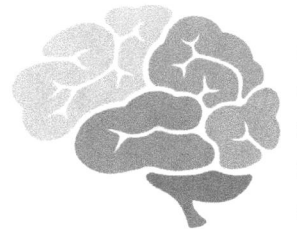

## Backed by Brain Science

Let's face it — nursing school can feel like trying to drink from a firehose. Between the jargon, the never-ending lists, and the sheer volume of information, it's easy to feel overwhelmed. That's exactly why the Made Easy series was born: to make the hard stuff stick without frying your brain. And while it might look fun and playful on the outside (hello, rhymes!), it's all built on rock-solid research from the nerdy world of educational psychology.

## 1. COGNITIVE LOAD THEORY

First up: Cognitive Load Theory. Fancy name, simple idea — your brain can only handle so much at once. When materials are too dense or packed with fluff, your working memory taps out. Educational psychologist John Sweller figured this out, and we took notes. That's why our poems give you the essentials only, in small, memorable doses. Less clutter, more clarity. (Sweller, 1988; Clark et al., 2006)

## 2. DUAL CODING THEORY

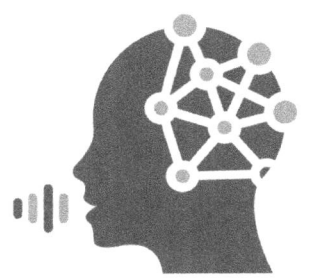

Then there's Dual Coding Theory, brought to us by Allan Paivio. He discovered that we remember things better when we learn them through both words and visuals. Our poems lean into this by using rhyme and rhythm to boost verbal memory — and bolded key terms, color coding, and clean formatting to give your visual brain a treat. Two paths to your brain = double the retention. (Paivio, 1986; Mayer, 2009)

## 3. ADVANCE ORGANIZERS

Psychologist David Ausubel believed that when we know how new info fits into what we already know, we learn faster. That's the beauty of our repeatable poem structure. Once you get the hang of the format, your brain relaxes — and focuses on what actually matters: the content. Think of it like a familiar playlist for your mind. (Ausubel, 1960)

## 4. MICROLEARNING

Our poems are also bite-sized by design, and that's no accident. Welcome to the world of microlearning — the idea that small, focused learning units are easier to digest and retain. This is a game-changer for busy, burnt-out students. Instead of cramming for hours, you can study just one medication, one skill, or one critical concept at a time. Snack-sized studying with full-course impact. (Hug, 2005; van den Berg & van den Berg, 2021)

## 5. SPACED REPETITION & RETRIEVAL PRACTICE

Last but definitely not least: spaced repetition and retrieval practice. These two learning powerhouses have proven time and again that the more often you recall information over time, the longer you'll remember it. Our poems are made for this. Easy to reread, perfect for flashcards, and fun enough to come back to (yes, we admitted it). Rinse and repeat — and retain. (Dunlosky et al., 2013)

So, yes — this method might look different than your typical textbook grind. That's the point. It's effective on purpose. Because learning tough topics shouldn't feel impossible. It should feel doable. Even a little fun. And with Made Easy, it totally is.

# Read it. Rhyme it. Remember it.

That's the Made Easy Method—a simple but powerful approach to mastering complex nursing material.

### START WITH THE BIG PICTURE

Before diving into individual medications, review the Mind Maps (via QR code). These quick-reference visuals give you the foundational understanding needed for any medication.

Included mind maps:
- The Life of a Drug in the Body (pharmacokinetics)
- Drug Classifications
- Common Side Effect Categories
- High-Risk Medication Categories
- Drug Schedules (I-V)
- Therapeutic Index & Drug Monitoring
- Common Drug Interactions
- Ways to Memorize Meds

These are perfect for test prep, concept review, and connecting the dots across drug types.

### USE THE MEMORY TRICKS & MNEMONICS

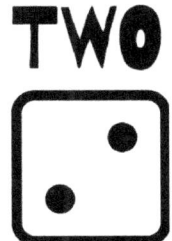

We've included 2 pages of mnemonic "cards" — visual reminders of popular phrases and acronyms students actually use (and remember!).

Cut them out, hang them up, or snap a pic to review on the go.

# THREE

## STUDY WITH PURPOSE

Don't just read — actively study.

As you go through each medication, we encourage you to highlight or underline using this color-coded system to instantly recognize what's what:

- ▇ Drug Classification & Names
- ▇ Mechanism of Action
- ▇ Indications
- ▇ Side Effects & Adverse Reactions
- ▇ Nursing Considerations
- ▇ Monitoring Requirements
- ▇ Patient & Caregiver Teaching Points
- ● Black Box Warnings
- ▇ Pediatric Considerations
- ● Drug Interactions

(Pro Tip: You don't need 10 highlighters — just make a little color key and underline or box with gel pens or colored pencils!)

## COMPLETE THE MIND MAP

# FOUR

Once you've highlighted, it's time to organize what you've learned. Use the Medication Mind Map Template in the back of the book to visually break down the drug:

- Class, MOA, Indications
- Side effects, warnings, teaching points
- Your favorite memory trick or mnemonic

This helps you actually process and remember what you just studied — way better than passive reading.

## FIVE

### TEST WHAT YOU KNOW

After each section, you'll find a QR code that takes you straight to a short NCLEX-style quiz hosted in Google Forms. These aren't just random practice questions — they're carefully crafted to test the most important takeaways from what you just read. But the real magic? <u>The rationales.</u> Whether you get the answer right or wrong, the quiz walks you through the why. Understanding the reasoning behind each answer helps you think like a nurse, not just a test-taker.

It's not about memorizing — it's about making connections, strengthening critical thinking, and applying your knowledge in real clinical scenarios. So take your time, review the rationales, and let them guide you from confusion to clarity.

# So don't just read these pages—
# *interact with them.*

### 📖 **Re**ad it. 🎵 **Rhy**me it. 🧠 **Re**member it.

That's how we make nursing Made Easy.

> "Nursing is an art: and if it is to be made an art, it requires an exclusive devotion as hard a preparation as any painter's or sculptor's work."
> - Florence Nightingale

# PHARMACOLOGY MIND MAPS

## COMMON DRUG INTERACTIONS

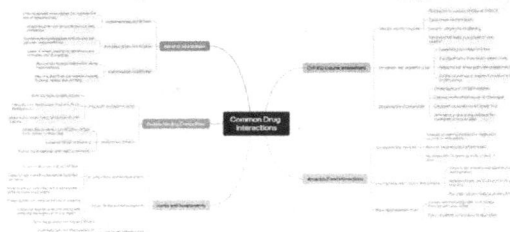

## THE LIFE OF A DRUG IN THE BODY

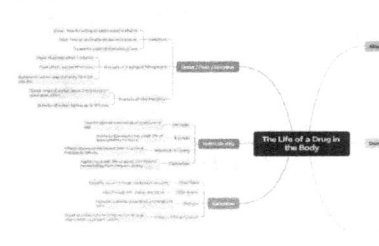

## DRUG CLASSIFICATIONS

## HIGH-RISK MEDICATION CATEGORIES

## DRUG SCHEDULES

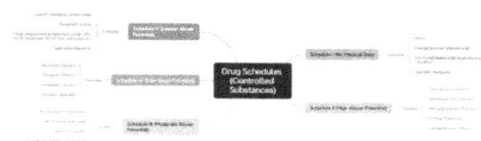

## THERAPEUTIC INDEX & DRUG MONITORING

## COMMON DRUG INTERACTIONS

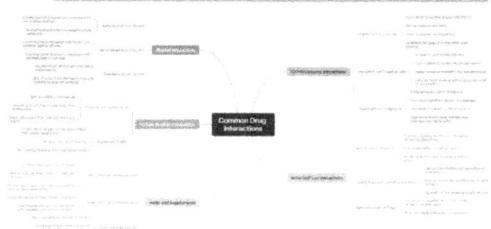

## WAYS TO MEMORIZE MEDICATIONS

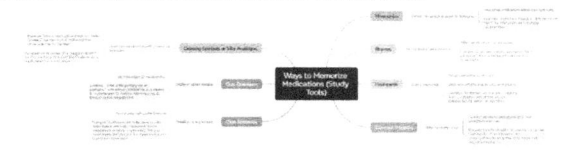

## SLUDGE
### CHOLINERGIC EFFECTS

**S**alivation, **L**acrimation, **U**rination, **D**iaphoresis, **G**I upset, **E**mesis

*Seen in cholinergic overdose or organophosphate poisoning.*

## ANTICHOLINERGIC
**Can't Pee, See, Spit, or Poop**

Blurred vision, Urinary retention, Dry mouth, Constipation

*Helps recall the hallmark side effects of anticholinergic medications.*

## NAMES OF INSULINS - **L.A.N.D.**

**L**antus = Long-acting
**A**pidra = Rapid-acting
**N**ovolog = Rapid-acting
**D**etemir = Long-acting

## BETA-BLOCKERS

"**LOL** Makes the Heart Rate Slow"

*All beta-blockers end in "-lol." They decrease heart rate and blood pressure by blocking beta-adrenergic receptors.*

## ACE INHIBITORS

"**-PRIL** Puts the Pressure Down"

*Pressure Reduced In Large vessels. They lower blood pressure by preventing angiotensin II formation.*

## CALCIUM CHANNEL BLOCKERS

"**V**ery **N**ice **D**rugs"
**V**erapamil, **N**ifedipine, **D**iltiazem

*These drugs dilate blood vessels and slow the heart rate, reducing workload on the heart.*

## DIURETICS

"**DIM** the Fluid Volume"

**D**iuretics, **I**ncrease, **M**icturition (urination)

*Loop diuretics (e.g., furosemide) or thiazides (e.g., hydrochlorothiazide) help reduce fluid volume, easing edema or hypertension.*

## ANTICOAGULANTS

"Heparin Works **FAST**, Coumadin **LASTS**"

*Heparin is for acute management; Warfarin for long-term prevention. Always monitor lab values (PTT for heparin, PT/INR for warfarin).*

## ANTIBIOTICS (PENICILLINS & CEPHALOSPORINS)

"Cross Allergy Alerts"

*All beta-blockers end in "-lol." They decrease heart rate and blood pressure by blocking beta-adrenergic receptors.*

## LIDOCAINE TOXICITY

"**SAMS**"
**S**lurred speech, **A**ltered central nervous system, **M**uscle twitching, **S**eizures

*Recognize signs of lidocaine toxicity.*

## MEDICATION ADMINISTRATION CHECKLIST

"**TRAMP**"

**T**ime, **R**oute, **A**mount, **M**edication, **P**atient

*Ensure the five rights of medication administration.*

## EMERGENCY DRUGS TO "**LEAN**" ON

**L**idocaine, **E**pinephrine, **A**tropine, **N**aloxone

*Common emergency medications administered via endotracheal tube.*

### VENTRICULAR ARRHYTHMIAS
**"PALS"**

Procainamide, Amiodarone, Lidocaine, Sotalol

*Medications used to treat ventricular arrhythmias.*

---

### ATRIAL ARRHYTHMIAS
**"ABCDE"**

Anticoagulants, Beta blockers, Calcium channel blockers, Digoxin, Electrocardioversion

*Treatment options for atrial arrhythmias.*

---

### MORPHINE SIDE EFFECTS
**"MORPHINE"**

Miosis, Out of it (sedation), Respiratory depression, Pneumonia (aspiration), Hypotension, Infrequency (constipation, urinary retention), Nausea, Emesis

---

### PARKINSON'S MEDICATIONS
**"ALBM"**

Amantadine, Levodopa, Bromocriptine, MAO-B inhibitors

*Drugs commonly used to manage Parkinson's disease.*

---

### THIAZIDES INDICATIONS
**"CHIC"**

Congestive heart failure, Hypertension, Insipidus (diabetes insipidus), Calcium calculi (kidney stones)

*Primary uses for thiazide diuretics.*

---

### BRADYCARDIA & HYPOTENSION
**"IDEA"**

Isoproterenol, Dopamine, Epinephrine, Atropine sulfate

*Medications used to manage bradycardia and hypotension.*

---

### STEROID SIDE EFFECTS
**"6 S's"**

Sugar - hyperglycemia, Soggy bones - osteoporosis, Sick - decreased immunity, Sad - depression, Salt - water and salt retention, Sex - decreased libido

---

### LOOP DIURETIC EFFECTS
**"LOOP"**

Lose sodium, Ototoxicity, Orthostatic hypotension, Potassium loss

*Highlights the primary effects and risks of loop diuretics.*

---

### ACE INHIBITOR SIDE EFFECTS
**"CAPTOPRIL"**

Cough, Angioedema, Proteinuria, Taste changes, Orthostatic hypotension, Pregnancy contraindication, Rash, Increased renin, Lower angiotensin II

---

### BETA-BLOCKER CONTRAINDICATIONS
**"ABCDE"**

Asthma, Block (heart block), COPD, Diabetes mellitus, Electrolyte (hyperkalemia)

*Highlights conditions where beta-blockers should be used cautiously or avoided.*

---

### GYNECOMASTIA
**"DISCO"**

Digitalis, Isoniazid, Spironolactone, Cimetidine, Oestrogens

*Identifies medications known to cause gynecomastia as a side effect.*

---

### TOXICOLOGICAL SEIZURES
**"OTIS CAMPBELL"**

Organophosphates, Tricyclic antidepressants, Isoniazid, Insulin, Sympathomimetics, Camphor, Cocaine, Amphetamines, Methylxanthines, PCP, Propoxyphene, Phenol, Propranolol, Benzodiazepine withdrawal, Botanicals, Ethanol withdrawal, Lithium, Lidocaine, Lindane, Lead

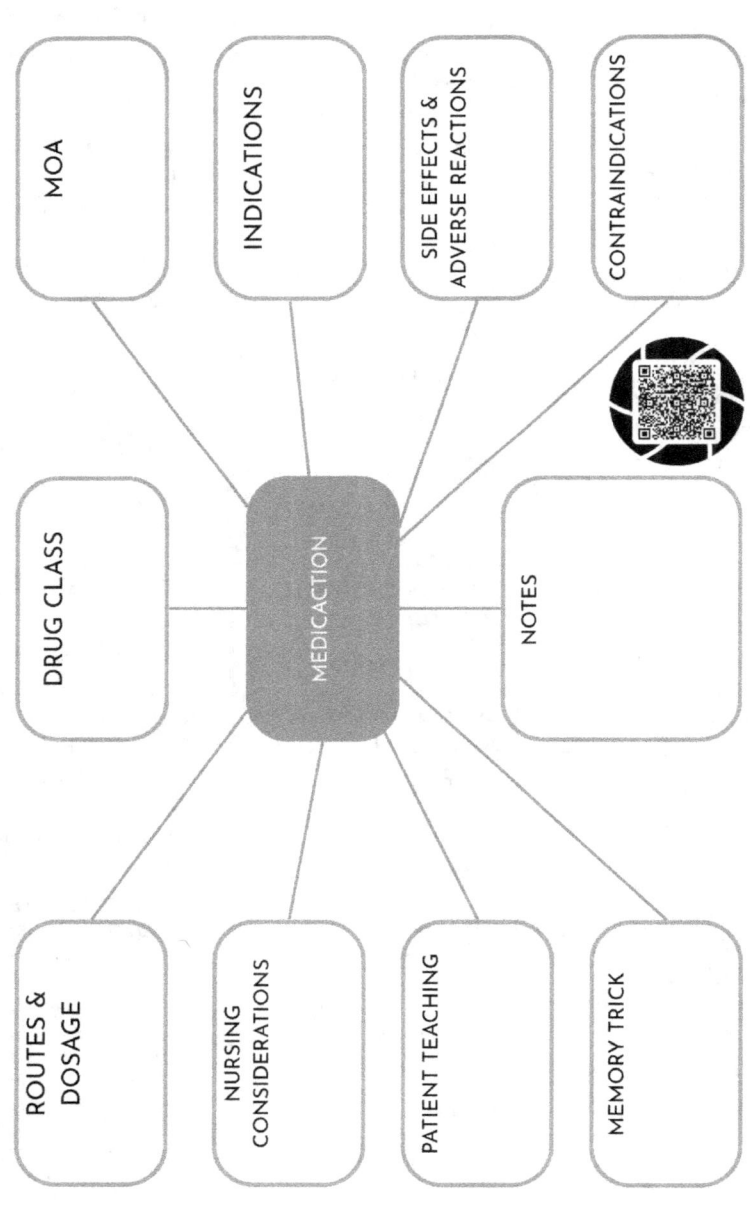

# Adalimumab (Humira)

*TNF-alpha Inhibitor – Monoclonal Antibody*

A biologic agent, a TNF-blocker,
For Crohn's and colitis, it's quite the shocker.
A monoclonal antibody in disguise,
It calms inflammation where trouble lies.
It blocks TNF, a cytokine bold,
That causes flare-ups uncontrolled.
So for IBD that's out of hand,
Adalimumab lends a steady hand.

Given subQ, not through the vein,
It helps to ease your patient's pain.
But watch for fever, chills, or rash—
Infections can come on in a flash.
Tuberculosis is a real concern,
So screen before you let it burn.
Also beware of Hep B flair,
And cancers in kids—nurses, beware.

Injection site may itch or swell,
And headache's common, patients tell.

They may feel tired, or catch the flu—
These are side effects we often view.
Teach them how to self-inject,
Rotate sites, and do a check:
Is the drug clear? No chunks inside?
Then it's good to go—arms open wide.

Monitor CBCs, LFTs too,
Watch for signs the liver's blue.
No live vaccines while it's in play,
And keep infections far away.
It can interact with other meds,
Like other TNF blockers—use your heads.
So nurses, stay alert and wise—
With Humira, safety saves lives.

# Albendazole (Albenza)

*Anthelmintic – Anti-parasitic Agent*

Albendazole fights the worms,
In tapeworm wars, it stands firm.
A benzimidazole, strong and sly,
It stops the bugs that wiggle by.
It binds to tubulin, halts their tracks,
Inhibits glucose—no energy packs.
From larvae deep to eggs so small,
It paralyzes and kills them all.

Used for *neurocysticercosis* brain,
And *hydatid disease* that causes pain.
It tackles roundworms, pinworms too—
A go-to med for a parasite crew.
But don't be fooled, side effects hide:
Liver enzymes climbing high tide,
Nausea, vomiting, belly aches,
Dizziness or rash—nursing stakes.

Start with food to aid absorption,
And reduce the GI disruption.

Teach to take the full regime,
Even if they start to seem...
Worm-free, clear, and doing great—
They must still medicate.

Liver tests must be in view,
Before and during treatment too.
CBCs for bone marrow drop,
If neutrophils fall, you might need to stop.
Pregnant patients? No, not yet—
It's teratogenic, a serious threat.
Contraceptives should be in play,
During and after the med's last day.

Interactions may come with cimetidine,
Or dexamethasone stepping in.
They raise the levels—keep that tracked,
So adverse risks don't sneak back.
So when parasites take their stance,
Albendazole gives no chance.
Nurse with care, prepare with might,
And help your patient win the fight.

# Alosetron (Lotronex)

*5-HT3 Receptor Antagonist – IBS Agent*

For women with IBS-D distress,
Alosetron helps the gut calm its mess.
It blocks 5-HT3 in the colon's domain,
To slow those spasms and ease the pain.
It works on nerves in the GI tract,
Where serotonin keeps things packed.
By dulling that signal, it helps reduce
Urgent stools and abdominal abuse.

Only for females with severe flares,
Who've tried all else and gotten nowhere.
It's not for bloating or mild frustration—
Only the toughest constipation-rotation.
But caution! This drug can turn the tide,
With **ischemic colitis** lurking inside.
So watch for signs like blood-stained stools,
Or pain that breaks the common rules.

Side effects include constipation's grip—
And not just mild, but severe and swift.

Fatigue and hemorrhoids may come too,
So monitor closely like nurses do.
It's a **REMS drug** with strict consent,
A signed agreement before it's sent.
Patients must know all the risks they take,
This isn't a med to use by mistake.

Avoid with drugs that slow the gut,
Like anticholinergics in the cut.
Fluvoxamine? No, avoid that pair—
It raises levels beyond what's fair.
Teaching points? Keep patients alert:
"Call your provider if you're hurt.
Blood in the toilet? Belly's tight?
That's not okay—get checked tonight."

So Lotronex, when used just right,
Can ease the pain and end the fight.
But tread with care, don't go too fast—
This GI med is built to last.

# Alpha-Galactosidase (Beano)

*Digestive Enzyme – Gas-Relief Supplement*

When beans and veggies make you bloat,
Alpha-galactosidase gets the vote.
Found in Beano, it breaks things down,
So gas and cramps don't stick around.
An enzyme that digests with grace
Oligosaccharides in your plate.
It helps your gut before the flare,
By stopping gas before it's there.

It's **not a drug**, but an OTC aid—
A supplement that's enzyme-made.
Take it **right before your meal** begins,
To help digestion from within.
No wild side effects to dread,
But rare reactions could be ahead:
Rash or itching in those allergic—
So caution's key, even if it's herbal-esque.

Teaching? Simple—use with food,
Not on its own or in a fasted mood.

Take with the **first bite** of each meal,

So it can work before you feel.

It's safe for most, but **not for galactosemia**,

As it can worsen that rare anemia.

So screen for that before the go—

Even mild risks, nurses should know.

Watch for labels—don't get burned:

It **won't help with lactose**, just be firm.

This one's for beans, grains, veggies deep—

Not dairy, sweets, or meats you eat.

No black box here, just patient cheer,

A gentler gut when Beano's near.

A handy fix for mealtime woes,

That helps digestion work and flow.

# Aluminum Hydroxide/Magnesium Hydroxide (Maalox, Mylanta)

*Antacid – Acid Neutralizer*

Heartburn flares and stomach aches,
Call for antacids to hit the brakes.
Maalox and Mylanta take the stage,
To soothe the burn and calm the rage.
Aluminum and magnesium blend,
To neutralize acid—bring relief, not end.
They work right **in the stomach's space**,
Raising pH to a gentler place.
Used for **GERD, indigestion, sour belly**,
They smooth the burn, reduce the jelly.
Also given for **ulcer pain**,
They coat the gut like gentle rain.
But watch the balance—side effects swap:
Aluminum can **constipate and stop**,
While magnesium speeds the other way,
Causing **diarrhea** some would say.
Chronic use can lead to trouble,
**Electrolytes off**, risk is double.

Too much magnesium? Think **low BP**,

**Bradycardia**, or lethargy.

Teaching tips? **Take after meals**,

Or when heartburn starts to steal your feels.

But don't take close to other pills—

It messes with absorption skills.

Watch **kidney function**—this is key,

Especially with **magnesium** running free.

Renal failure? Then say no—

These metals build and overflow.

No black box warning here today,

But educate your folks each way:

Don't treat long-term without a check,

Or you might miss a GI wreck.

It interacts with meds like iron,

Tetracycline and dig, be warnin'.

Separate doses by **2 hours or more**,

So other meds can do their chore.

So Maalox and Mylanta, soft and fast,

Relieve the burn, but effects don't last.

Teach with care and monitor signs,

For acid meds that work in time.

# Alvimopan (Entereg)

*Peripheral μ-Opioid Receptor Antagonist – Postoperative Ileus Agent*

When bowels stall from surgery's strain,

Alvimopan helps restore the train.

A gut-specific, clever tool,

To wake the bowels and break the rule.

It blocks **mu-opioid** sites in the gut,

Where post-op meds can keep things shut.

But it **won't cross into the brain**,

So pain relief can still remain.

Used in hospitals short-term stay,

To speed up GI motility's way.

It's for bowel surgery patients in need,

When opioids slow their gut's good speed.

Watch for side effects, mild at best:

**Hypokalemia**, or back pain, rest.

Flatulence, dyspepsia may appear,

Or urinary retention—keep that clear.

**REMS drug** with rules in place—

Only hospitals can start this race.
Max of **15 doses** is the line,
More than that is **not benign**.
Black box warning? Yes, it's bold:
**MI risk** if long-term use unfolds.
So nurses monitor heart and bowels,
And flag chest pain or cardiac growls.

No use for patients who've had **opioids chronic**,
The risk of MI becomes more tonic.
Avoid if they've used opioids pre-op—
That's a contraindication—hard stop.
Check **electrolytes** and **bowel signs**,
Monitor output and all stool times.
Teach the purpose—what it's for,
And when they'll stop (it's not for more!).

No OTC or take-home dose,
This med is hospital use only—close.
But when it's time to help guts move,
Alvimopan helps find the groove.

# Aprepitant (Emend)

*Neurokinin-1 (NK1) Receptor Antagonist – Antiemetic*

When chemo makes the stomach churn,
And nausea starts to twist and burn,
Aprepitant steps in to defend—
This antiemetic called **Emend**.
It blocks **NK1 receptors** tight,
Where **substance P** would stir a fight.
So vomiting signals can't take hold—
It keeps that gag reflex controlled.

Used with **chemo and post-op care**,
To stop the nausea waiting there.
It's part of triple anti-nausea crews—
With **ondansetron** and **dexamethasone** too.
Side effects? They're mostly mild:
**Fatigue**, **hiccups**, or dizzy wild.
**Diarrhea** and **anorexia** may occur,
And liver enzymes may slightly stir.

Teaching? Take it **one hour before**
Chemo starts—timing is the core.

Then follow dosing day by day,
To keep that nausea far away.
Monitor **LFTs** for liver strain,
Especially if there's right-side pain.
Check for drug interactions too—
It **alters CYP3A4** in you.

So **warfarin**, **midazolam**, and **BCP**
May work too strong—or not effectively.
Warn women to use back-up plans,
If on birth control while this stands.
No black box warning—but still be wise,
And monitor patients with thoughtful eyes.
This med's a friend when chemo hits,
And nausea just won't call it quits.

So nurses, prep the Emend dose,
To keep those stomach flares more close.
With teaching clear and care in hand,
Aprepitant will help them stand.

# Atropine (Atropine Ophthalmic)

*Anticholinergic – Mydriatic & Cycloplegic Agent*

When eyes need rest or pupil wide,
Atropine drops are placed inside.
They block the **muscarinic sites**,
To **dilate pupils** and blur the sights.
This **anticholinergic** goes straight to the eye,
To stop constriction and let light fly.
It also **paralyzes the lens's motion**,
So focusing becomes slow like ocean.

Used in **uveitis**, to ease the pain,
Or **before exams** in the vision lane.
Also helpful in lazy eye fights—
**Penalizes** the stronger sights.
Side effects? Well, here's a few:
**Blurred vision** is the biggest clue.
**Photophobia**—light feels bright,
And **dry mouth** if it drains just right.

In rare cases, **tachycardia** might start,
So monitor those with a sensitive heart.

**Systemic absorption** in kids is real,

So apply **punctal pressure**—that's the deal.

Teach them not to touch the tip,

Or germs and bugs might take a trip.

And after drops, **press the inner eye**,

To keep the med where it should lie.


No black box, but **extra care**

With kids and elders—be aware.

Toxicity signs include confusion,

Hot, dry skin and disillusion.

It can **interact with other anticholinergics**,

So be cautious with combos—it's not allegoric.

And if your patient wears soft contacts,

Wait **15 minutes**—that's a fact.


So when pupils must be still and wide,

Atropine drops are on your side.

Just dose with care, and watch the signs,

For this little drop has powerful lines.

# Azathioprine (Imuran)

*Immunosuppressant – Purine Antagonist*

Azathioprine, immune control,
Suppresses flares to calm the whole.
A purine blocker through and through,
It halts cell growth, both bad and new.
For **ulcerative colitis** and **Crohn's disease**,
It keeps the gut inflammation at ease.
Also used in **transplants** too,
To stop rejection from breaking through.
It halts the DNA being made,
In fast-dividing cells it laid.
So T and B cells slow their might—
And lessen autoimmune fight.
Side effects you need to note:
**Bone marrow suppression** gets the vote.
**Leukopenia, thrombocytopenia** too,
**Infection risk** is rising through.
Watch for **fever, sore throat, chills**,
These might mean bugs break through the stills.
**Hepatotoxicity** can rise,
So **LFTs** need watching eyes.

There's a **black box warning** bold and clear:

**Malignancy risks** are drawing near—

Especially **lymphoma**, so don't ignore,

This drug is not a med to pour.

Also watch the **TPMT gene**—

Low levels mean tox will be seen.

A test before may guide the plan,

And help adjust for each lifespan.

Interactions come into play

With **allopurinol**—dose down right away.

Avoid live vaccines while on this med,

Immunity's too low instead.

Teach patients signs they need to track:

Bleeding gums or bruises back,

Dark urine, yellow skin or eyes—

Liver strain is no disguise.

Take it **with food** to ease the gut,

Though nausea still might show up but...

If taken daily as advised,

It tames the gut and quiets the cries.

So for autoimmune flares that burn,

Azathioprine helps them turn.

# Barium Sulfate Suspension
*Radiographic Contrast Agent – Diagnostic Aid*

Not a drug to heal or mend,
But **barium** helps diagnostics lend.
A chalky drink or enema flow,
To make the GI tract clearly show.
It's **inert**, not absorbed at all—
Just fills the gut from throat to hall.
Used in **X-rays, CTs**, and scopes,
To map out ulcers, leaks, or slopes.
From **esophagus to rectal end**,
It outlines shapes that twists and bend.
Detects **strictures, masses, blockage**, too—
And shows what's stuck or passing through.
Side effects are pretty rare,
But **nausea, cramps**, and **fullness** flare.
If swallowed wrong, **aspiration's** bad—
Pneumonitis makes lungs feel sad.
Biggest risk? **Bowel perforation**—
So **don't give** if that's the situation.
Never use when tears may hide,
Or in **obstruction**, step aside.

Teaching? Easy—start with this:

**NPO** before to not miss.

Then warn them: "You'll feel thick inside,"

And "yes, your poop turns chalky-white."

They might feel bloated or need to strain—

Push **fluids** to flush the gut again.

And if no bowel move in two days,

Call the doc—it's time to appraise.

There's **no black box** for this chalky brew,

But nurses still have things to do:

Check for allergies, **GI tears**,

**Aspiration risk**, and all those flares.

No drug-drug mix, but timing's tight—

It may delay meds taken that night.

Space them out to play it safe,

And document the test in place.

So when the GI map's unclear,

Barium brings that picture near.

It coats the walls and lights the way,

So radiologists can say what they say.

# Bifidobacterium Infantis (Align)

*Probiotic – GI Flora Regulator*

A friendly bug in capsule form,
Bifidobacterium keeps guts warm.
Align is how it's sold and named—
For GI health, it's widely acclaimed.
It's not a drug, but **probiotic aid**,
To help the gut stay well-behaved.
It adds good flora back inside,
When antibiotics wipe the tide.

It works by **balancing the gut**,
So bloating, gas, and pain are cut.
Great for **IBS**, some may find,
It calms the cramps and soothes the mind.
Side effects are **mild to rare**:
**Gas**, **bloating**, maybe air.
In those immune-compromised,
Use with caution—risk is sized.

**No black box** warnings on this one,
But nurses still have work to be done.

If patients have **fever or chills** arise,
Stop the use and reassess wise.
Teach to take it **daily, same time**,
With or without food—it's fine.
But don't mix with piping hot,
That heat will kill what Align's got.

Monitor outcomes over weeks,
For gut relief the patient seeks.
And don't expect results too fast—
It takes time for flora to last.
No major drug interactions here,
But keep immune concerns near.
It's a **dietary supplement**, clear—
Not FDA-checked like drugs appear.

So when guts are loud and out of line,
Align may help them feel just fine.
Restore the peace, reduce the strife,
And bring back balance to gut life.

# Bisacodyl (Dulcolax)

*Stimulant Laxative – Bowel Evacuant*

When bowels stall and don't obey,
Bisacodyl helps clear the way.
It works by **stimulating nerves** inside,
To get the colon to open wide.
It **increases motility** with a jolt,
To push that stool out like a bolt.
It also draws in water too,
For softer stools to pass on through.
Used for **constipation**, short and light,
Or pre-op prep the day or night.
Also given before GI scans,
To help clear bowels per the plans.
Side effects? You might see:
**Cramping**, **diarrhea**, urgency.
**Electrolyte loss** if used too long,
**Hypokalemia** sings its song.
No black box warning, but still a flag—
Don't let chronic use become a drag.
Dependence grows when taken daily,
So teach them to avoid it gaily.

Nursing tips? Give on time—
**Oral: at night**, for morning's climb.
**Suppository: in 15 minutes**,
Quick relief once it begins it.
**Enteric coating** must stay intact,
No chewing, breaking—keep the pact.
Don't take with **milk or antacids**,
They'll break the shell and cause upsets.
Interactions? Not too wide,
But **diuretics** may coincide—
Together they could drain K+,
So monitor labs and don't just guess.
Teach hydration's key, of course,
And **fiber** helps the natural force.
Lifestyle first, then lax when stuck,
Don't overuse or press your luck.
So Dulcolax, in pill or poke,
Gives the bowels a little poke.
But used with care and nurse insight,
It gets things moving just right.

# Bismuth Subsalicylate (Pepto-Bismol, Kaopectate)

*Antidiarrheal / Antiulcer Agent – GI Protectant & Salicylate*

When tummies grumble, churn, or squirm,
This pink elixir helps confirm:
Relief is near—just take a dose,
And soothe that gut from end to gross.
It coats the stomach, kills some bugs,
Absorbs the toxins, calms the lugs.
**Antisecretory, antimicrobial** blend,
For diarrhea, ulcers, or heartburn to end.
It slows the gut and kills H. pylori,
Part of **quadruple therapy's** glory.
For **nausea, gas, and traveler's plight**,
It brings the belly back to right.
Side effects? A few to flag:
**Black tongue** and **stools**—don't let that drag.
It's harmless, yes, but quite a sight—
Still, tell the patient, "That's all right."
But **salicylate** means caution bold,
For **kids with fever**, don't be sold.

**Reye's syndrome** risk is why we pause—
No use in flu or chickenpox clause.
Also watch for **tinnitus ring**,
A sign that levels may start to swing.
Avoid with **aspirin, NSAIDs** too,
Bleeding risks can rise on cue.
Teach to **shake the bottle well**,
And **space out meds** so all goes well.
**No more than 8 doses/day**,
Or side effects may come to play.
**Don't give with anticoagulants** near—
It amplifies the bleed you fear.
And **renal issues?** Use with care—
Salicylates can worsen there.
Pregnant? Skip it—play it safe.
Lactating moms should find another waif.
And don't forget the chalky coat—
May bind to meds and make them float.
So Pepto-Bismol, pink and proud,
Calms the guts that groan out loud.
With proper teaching, dose, and checks,
It earns its place on nursing decks.

# Budesonide (Entocort EC, Uceris)

*Corticosteroid – GI Anti-inflammatory*

When inflammation flares in the gut,
Budesonide can calm the rut.
A **steroid** with a local aim,
To cool the colon's burning flame.
It works by **suppressing cytokine calls**,
Reducing swelling in GI walls.
Less systemic than pred or the rest,
It targets the gut—where it works best.
Used in **Crohn's** and **ulcerative colitis** too,
For mild to moderate flares breaking through.
Entocort for **ileum and right-side colon**,
Uceris when **UC** is rollin'.
Side effects? Though less than some,
They still may sneak up when they come:
**Headache, nausea**, mood swings wild,
**Acne, indigestion**, in adult or child.
**Adrenal suppression** is still in play,
So taper off, don't quit in a day.
Watch for signs the body's stressed—
Like fatigue or BP that's less.

No black box, but stay aware—

**Infection risk** is always there.

Monitor **bone density** and eyes,

With long-term use, that's where risk lies.

It interacts with **CYP3A4**—

So drugs like **ketoconazole** may do more.

**Grapefruit juice?** Just say no,

It can raise the steroid's flow.

Teach patients to **swallow whole**, not crushed,

And take **in the morning**, not in a rush.

Don't use with antacids right away,

They change release and delay the play.

It's not a rescue—don't confuse,

It's for **maintenance**, not urgent use.

And while it's more "gut-safe" than some,

Still monitor labs as time goes on.

So Budesonide, calm and clean,

A focused fix for bowel spleen.

With clear instructions and steady plan,

It helps the gut heal where it can.

# Calcium Carbonate (Tums)

*Antacid / Calcium Supplement – Acid Neutralizer*

When acid creeps and starts to rise,
Tums steps in as a quick disguise.
A **base** that calms the burn with grace,
It neutralizes stomach's fiery place.
Calcium carbonate's the name,
And **heartburn relief** is its main claim.
Also used when **calcium's low**,
It boosts the bones and helps them grow.
Mechanism? It's plain and fast:
It **buffers acid** as it's passed.
No fancy pathways deep inside,
Just **direct neutralizing**—gut-wide.
Side effects? Not many feared,
But **constipation** can appear.
In higher doses or overuse,
**Hypercalcemia** may let loose.
**Milk-alkali syndrome** is rare but true—
With nausea, stones, and mental blue.
So **don't exceed the daily dose**,
Even if the burn is close.

Nursing tips? **Give after meals**,

Or when reflux tries its deals.

Teach them not to pop like candy,

Even if the chalk feels handy.

Don't take with **iron** or **tetracyclines**,

Or other meds with tight designs.

It binds them up and blocks their role,

So **space by 1–2 hours** is the goal.

Teach patients signs of calcium high:

**Muscle weakness**, **stones**, or dry.

And if on **thiazides**, be aware—

They raise calcium in the blood somewhere.

**No black box**, but use with care,

Especially with chronic flare.

It's not a fix for ulcers deep,

Or chronic GERD that doesn't sleep.

So Tums can bring fast, short relief,

But long-term use may cause some grief.

With nurse-led guidance and spacing clear,

Calcium carbonate's a friend, not fear.

# Castor Oil

*Stimulant Laxative – Natural Bowel Evacuant*

From nature's plant and ancient lore,
Castor oil opens the GI door.
A **stimulant laxative**, bold and quick,
It clears the bowels with one strong kick.
It's broken down in the upper gut,
To **ricinoleic acid**—that's the cut.
That compound irritates the bowels inside,
Increasing **motility far and wide**.

Used for **constipation**, stubborn and slow,
Or sometimes **bowel prep** before you go.
But not for daily use or play—
Dependence risk grows day by day.
Side effects may cramp your style:
**Nausea**, **diarrhea**, for a while.
**Electrolyte imbalance** can appear,
So hydration's key when dosing's near.

Avoid it in **pregnancy**, full stop—
It may cause **uterine contractions to pop**.

No black box warning, but heed the call:

It's not for chronic use at all.

Teach patients to **take it on an empty gut**,

With juice to mask the taste somewhat.

It works in **2 to 6 hours flat**,

So stay near toilets—don't forget that.

Not for kids unless the doc agrees,

And not with meds that dehydrate with ease.

**Loop diuretics**, for example,

Can make the body's balance scramble.

So castor oil, though natural-made,

Deserves the caution nurses trade.

Teach with care, observe the signs,

And clear the gut within safe lines.

# Cholestyramine (Questran)

*Bile Acid Sequestrant – Antidiarrheal / Lipid-Lowering Agent*

When bile salts irritate the gut,
Cholestyramine helps shut that rut.
A **bile acid binder** through and through,
It traps those salts and pulls them through.
Used for **bile acid diarrhea** that stays,
And **cholestasis-related itchy days**.
Also helps **lower LDL**,
In lipid control, it does quite well.
It **binds bile acids** in the gut,
Prevents their reabsorption rut.
The liver pulls from cholesterol stores,
To make more bile and open doors.
But don't forget—it's not absorbed,
So side effects come from GI orb:
**Constipation** leads the pack,
**Bloating**, **nausea**, flatulence back.
It may reduce the body's grab
Of **fat-soluble vitamins A, D, E, K lab**.
So supplements might be advised,

Especially if long-term used or prized.

Nursing tips? Teach timing right:

**Other meds should take a flight—**

**1 hour before or 4 hours after,**

So absorption's not a disaster.

Mix powder with **juice or soup,**

Not dry—don't make them jump through hoops.

Tell them it might take some tries,

To find the mix their gut complies.

No black box warning here to see,

But use with care in **GI disease.**

Avoid in patients with **complete obstruction,**

Or bowel motility reduction.

Watch **triglycerides**, if they're high,

Questran might send them to the sky.

So check those labs before you start,

And keep that lipid panel chart.

So cholestyramine's gritty and true,

Binding bile to help you through.

With patient teaching and thoughtful plan,

It soothes the gut and takes a stand.

# Cimetidine (Tagamet)

*H2 Receptor Antagonist – Acid Reducer*

When stomach acid flows too strong,
Cimetidine helps right the wrong.
A **histamine blocker**, H2 type,
It calms the burn and soothes the gripe.
It blocks H2 receptors in the gut,
So acid pumps don't open up.
Less acid means less ulcer pain,
And healing can begin again.
Used for **GERD**, **ulcers**, and reflux flare,
And **Zollinger-Ellison**, though that's rare.
Also helps prevent stress ulcer strain,
In patients ill or under strain.
Side effects? A mixed array:
**Headache**, **diarrhea**, come to play.
But watch for **gynecomastia** in men—
Hormonal changes now and then.
It may cause **CNS confusion**, too,
Especially in the frail or ICU.
Dizziness, restlessness—take note,
And reduce the dose for age and bloat.

No black box warning, but be aware:

**Liver and kidney function** need care.

Adjust the dose if either is low,

And monitor labs as symptoms go.

A **CYP450 inhibitor**, bold and proud—

It messes with drugs in a crowd.

**Warfarin, phenytoin, theophylline,**

Might rise too high if mixed within.

So space out meds and **check levels close,**

When using Cimetidine in the dose.

Also avoid with **antacids near,**

Give it **two hours apart,** keep it clear.

Teach patients to **avoid smoking**, too—

It cuts the med's effect in you.

And eat bland foods to help repair,

The GI tract and ulcers there.

So Tagamet can calm the flame,

When acid's wild and causing pain.

But nurses know to guard the path,

And monitor all in Cimetidine's wrath.

# Ciprofloxacin (Cipro)

*Fluoroquinolone Antibiotic – Broad-Spectrum Antibacterial*

When nasty bugs take hold within,
Ciprofloxacin fights to win.
A **fluoroquinolone**, sharp and wide,
It stops bacteria from dividing inside.
It blocks **DNA gyrase** in the cell,
Halts replication and growth as well.
Used for **UTIs**, **GI infections**, too,
And **traveler's diarrhea** passing through.
Also treats **diverticulitis** flair,
And **typhoid fever** if it's there.
It fights **gram-negatives** best of all,
But gram-positive bugs may heed the call.
Side effects can get intense—
**Tendon rupture** makes the most sense.
So if there's **pain in heel or joint**,
Stop the med and make the point.
**QT prolongation** leads the list,
So monitor ECG if risk exists.
**Photosensitivity**, GI upset—
And **mental status changes** you may get.

There's a **black box warning** here,
For **tendinitis** and rupture fear.
Also for **peripheral neuropathy**,
And **CNS effects** like anxiety.
Avoid in **myasthenia gravis** cases,
It worsens weakness in those spaces.
And **kids under 18?** Use with care—
Unless there's no better option there.
Nursing tips? Give with water glass,
And **don't take with milk, antacids, or brass.**
Calcium, zinc, and iron bind,
And leave absorption far behind.
Space out from **vitamins or dairy**,
To keep absorption strong and airy.
Teach them to **finish every dose**,
Even if symptoms have mostly closed.
Monitor for **superinfections** too,
Like **C. diff diarrhea** breaking through.
And check for **renal dosing** needs,
Especially in elders or complex feeds.
So Cipro's strong and broad and tough,
But not without its side effect stuff.

# Colesevelam (Welchol)

*Bile Acid Sequestrant – Lipid-Lowering & Antidiarrheal Agent*

Colesevelam comes to play,
When lipids rise or guts dismay.
A **bile acid binder** mild and clean,
It lowers **LDL** behind the scene.
It traps bile acids in the gut,
So more is made to fill the cut.
And since the liver pulls cholesterol down,
It helps to shrink that lipid crown.
Also used for **type 2 diabetes**,
To smooth out post-meal sugar rises.
And sometimes helps in **IBS-D**,
To slow the stool and bring some peace.
Side effects are mostly GI-based:
**Constipation**, bloating, gas displaced.
Rarely, **hypoglycemia** may show,
When paired with meds that drop it low.
No **black box warning**, but don't delay—
Teach to take it the proper way.
**With food** and water, fully mixed,

Or those GI woes may get affixed.

Teach them to **swallow whole, not crushed**,

And space out other meds—they'll get flushed.

**4 hours apart** is what we say,

Or absorption gets in the way.

It's not absorbed—just acts inside,

So few systemic effects abide.

But still, check **blood sugar and fats**,

And warn of stools that might fall flat.

No use in **bowel obstruction zones**,

Or those with **triglycerides over 500 zones**.

This drug may raise those levels high,

So monitor labs and don't just try.

Pregnancy safe and generally kind,

Welchol's gentle for the gut and mind.

But still a binder through and through,

So timing meds is key to do.

So Colesevelam, chalky friend,

Helps cholesterol descend.

With patient teaching and space in mind,

It's one the gut can learn to find.

# Dexlansoprazole (Dexilant)

*Proton Pump Inhibitor (PPI) – Acid Reducer*

When acid creeps both day and night,
Dexlansoprazole sets things right.
A **PPI**, it shuts the gate
On acid pumps that over-create.
It blocks the **H⁺/K⁺ ATPase** line,
In gastric walls where acids dine.
Reduces acid, heals the sore,
In **GERD**, **erosions**, and even more.
What makes Dexilant a bit unique?
Its **dual release** gives a longer peak.
So once-a-day can do the trick,
For symptoms mild or reflux thick.
Side effects? Some to track:
**Headache**, **nausea**, **diarrhea** back.
**Flatulence**, cough, or stomach pain—
And long-term use? That's a different lane.
Prolonged use brings **fracture risk**,
And **low magnesium**, so don't dismiss.
Watch for **B12 deficiency**, too,
Especially if used past a year or two.

**No black box warning**, but nurses know,

To monitor bones if years go.

And teach patients not to miss,

The signs of **hypocalcemia's** twist.

Drug interactions may arise

With **warfarin**, **dig**, or antifungals' ties.

Also affects **pH-dependent absorption**,

So check if meds need acid for function.

Take it **without regard to meals**,

Thanks to how its coating seals.

But stay consistent every day,

To keep those reflux flares at bay.

Teach them not to crush or chew—

That special capsule's built for you.

And if they take **antacids**, wait—

A gap of time is always great.

So Dexilant works deep inside,

Where gastric pumps would otherwise hide.

With guidance, labs, and timing keen,

It keeps the reflux calm and clean.

# Dicyclomine (Bentyl)

*Anticholinergic / Antispasmodic – GI Smooth Muscle Relaxant*

When bowels cramp and twist with pain,
Dicyclomine calms the strain.
An **anticholinergic**, smooth and sly,
It quiets spasms that make guts cry.
It blocks **acetylcholine's command**,
So muscles stop their squeezing stand.
Used for **IBS** with cramps and flare,
It brings relief from urgent care.

**Oral or IM**, but never IV—
The fast route's not for safety, see?
Take before meals, not on the run,
So it can work before things begun.
Side effects? Oh yes, a list:
**Dry mouth**, **blurred vision**, can't resist.
**Drowsiness, dizziness**, may appear,
So warn them not to drive too near.

**Urinary retention**, heat intolerance too,

Especially in heat, be cautious—true.

Elderly may feel **confused**,

So lower doses must be used.

**No black box**, but still take care—

Anticholinergic risks are there.

Avoid in those with **BPH**,

**Glaucoma**, or **myasthenia gravis**, please.

Teach patients this is for cramps, not gas,

And won't help flares that quickly pass.

It works best on **muscle pain**,

Not loose stool from another strain.

Check for meds that do the same—

Other **anticholinergics** fan the flame.

Additive effects may come too fast,

So check that full med list to last.

So Dicyclomine, gentle stop,

On bowel spasms that flip and flop.

With nursing care and clear advice,

It soothes the gut like something nice.

# Dimenhydrinate (Dramamine)

*Antihistamine – Antiemetic / Motion Sickness Agent*

When motion brings a queasy ride,
Dimenhydrinate turns the tide.
A **first-gen antihistamine**, strong and true,
It blocks **H1 receptors** to rescue you.
It also calms the **vestibular** sway,
To keep the nausea far away.
Used for **motion sickness**, **vertigo**, too,
And nausea that the body threw.

It kicks in quick—so take **before**
That cruise or flight or winding tour.
**Oral or IM**, the form may vary,
For travelers nervous or unwary.
Side effects? The usual crew:
**Drowsiness**, **dry mouth**, maybe a few
**Blurred vision**, **constipation**, dry eyes—
That's anticholinergic in disguise.

In kids or elders, extra care,
It may cause **paradoxical flair**—

Agitation instead of sleep,
So monitor if their calm won't keep.
No black box, but don't ignore
**Sedation risks**, especially more
If taken with **alcohol**, **opioids**, too—
That combo knocks the CNS askew.

Avoid with **glaucoma**, **BPH**,
Or **asthma**, where it may cause clash.
And take care with the driving crew—
This sleepy pill can hinder view.
Teach to take it **30 minutes ahead**
Of travel, motion, or boat-bed dread.
And space it out **every 4 to 6**,
But don't exceed the dosing mix.

So Dramamine, small and strong,
Keeps you steady all ride long.
With patient teaching and heads-up view,
You'll help them make it safely through.

# Diphenoxylate/Atropine (Lomotil)

*Antidiarrheal – Opioid Derivative with Anticholinergic*

When diarrhea runs too fast,
Lomotil helps to make it last.
A combo drug that slows the gut,
So watery stools are safely shut.
**Diphenoxylate**, the opioid star,
Slows peristalsis near and far.
**Atropine**'s added—not for flair,
But to stop abuse with side effects there.
Used for **acute diarrhea** tough,
When diet and fluids aren't enough.
Not for long-term daily use—
Just short-term help to call a truce.
Side effects? A mixed bouquet:
**Drowsiness**, **dry mouth**, and blurry sway.
**Constipation**, **nausea**, dizzy spins—
And in high doses, **euphoria** begins.
**Atropine adds anticholinergic tone**,
So **tachycardia**, **urine retention** might be shown.
And in kids or elders? Extra warning—
CNS effects can come without warning.

**No black box,** but listen here:

**Toxicity** risk is very clear.

Respiratory depression may occur,

Especially in children—watch for sure.

**Controlled substance - Schedule V,**

So teach your patients not to drive.

It acts like opioids in disguise,

So misuse risk is on the rise.

Avoid with **MAOIs**, sedative meds,

Or **alcohol**, which amplifies sleepy heads.

And teach about overdose signs—

**Pinpoint pupils**, slowed-down lines.

Take with food or without—it's fine,

But follow dosing line by line.

And **don't exceed 8 tabs a day**,

Or side effects may come to play.

So Lomotil helps the bowels behave,

But isn't one to freely crave.

With cautious use and nurse insight,

It turns loose stools from flight to right.

# Docusate Sodium (Colace)

*Stool Softener – Emollient Laxative*

When straining feels like way too much,
And stools are dry, compact, and such,
Docusate helps things slide with grace—
A gentle softener in the race.
It's not a lax that makes you run,
But **pulls in water**, one by one.
It softens stool, so it can pass,
Without the cramps or urgency gas.

Used for those who just had birth,
Or surgery near the lower girth.
Also for **MI patients**, post-op days,
To ease the strain in safer ways.
Side effects? They're rare but known:
**Diarrhea**, **cramps**, if too much is shown.
Sometimes **throat irritation** may come near,
If liquid forms aren't chased with cheer.

No black box warning here to fear,
But nurses still must make things clear:

It's not for treating sudden blockage,

Or those with **nausea, vomiting, or cramp collage**.

Teach them it takes a **day or two**,

To see results come pushing through.

Hydration is the key to win—

No water? Then it won't begin.

Avoid long-term daily dose,

Without the doctor's planned approach.

And don't use with **mineral oil**,

They interact and may cause toil.

Safe in pregnancy, widely used,

But still with teaching not confused:

It helps prevent—not treat—delay,

So use it right and not halfway.

So Colace softens, kind and slow,

A nurse's favorite, mild in flow.

With patient care and fluids in hand,

It keeps things moving as they planned.

# Eluxadoline (Viberzi)

*Mixed Opioid Receptor Modulator – IBS-D Agent*

For bowels that dash without control,
Eluxadoline helps console.
Viberzi's name, it slows the tide,
When **IBS-D** won't let things slide.
It works on **opioid receptors three**—
**Mu and kappa**, to slow the spree.
But **delta's blocked**, a unique twist,
To ease the pain without full risk.
Used for **irritable bowels, diarrhea-based**,
When urgency must be erased.
It quiets spasms, firms the stool,
And brings the gut back into rule.
Side effects? There's quite a few—
**Nausea**, **constipation**, cramps come through.
**Dizziness**, and **elevated enzymes**,
So check the liver at regular times.
**Black box warning**—don't dismiss:
**Pancreatitis** is a risk.
Especially in patients with no gallbladder,
That side effect can truly shatter.

Avoid in those who **drink too much**,
Or with liver disease and such.
No gallbladder? Then say no—
The risk is far too high to go.
Also avoid in **GI obstruction**,
Or **sphincter of Oddi** dysfunction.
And **those with biliary duct disease**
Could trigger pain that won't appease.
Nursing tips? Take **twice a day**,
With **food** to help it go the way.
Monitor for belly pain,
And stop if pancreatitis starts to gain.
**Controlled substance—Schedule IV**,
So teach your patients to want no more.
Don't share, don't double up the pill,
Use as prescribed or face the chill.
So Viberzi helps the bowels behave,
When IBS-D won't let them stay.
With teaching clear and risks in sight,
You'll help your patient feel just right.

# Erythromycin (Erythrocin)

*Macrolide Antibiotic – Prokinetic & Antibacterial Agent*

Erythromycin, classic name,
An **antibiotic** of old-school fame.
It stops the bugs by halting build—
**Blocks 50S ribosomes**, bacteria chilled.
Used for **GI bugs**, like **H. pylori**,
Or **gastroparesis**—a different story.
Because it mimics **motilin's call**,
It helps the stomach empty all.
So not just for bugs, but for the flow,
It helps the sluggish GI go.
But it's off-label when used that way—
Still, nurses see it save the day.
Side effects? Let's take a peek:
**Nausea**, **vomiting**, taste may tweak.
**Abdominal pain** is pretty common,
And **diarrhea** might keep things hummin'.
More serious? **QT prolongation**—
A risk for those with heart sensation.
**Torsades de Pointes** can be a fear,
So monitor EKGs clear.

**Hepatotoxicity** may arise,
Especially with IV in high-size.
So check those **LFTs** in time,
And watch for **jaundice**, pain, or grime.
**No black box warning**, but be wise—
The risk for arrhythmias can surprise.
And **drug interactions** lead the list,
It's a **CYP3A4** inhibitor twist.
So **statins, warfarin, carbamazepine**,
May spike or drop if you're not keen.
Avoid **with pimozide or ergot meds**,
Or else those side effects raise their heads.
Teach patients to take on **empty belly**,
With water clear, not toast or jelly.
Unless GI upset comes in play,
Then food is fine to keep it at bay.
So erythromycin, dual in kind,
Treats infections and gets things aligned.
But monitor heart and liver too,
And space out meds if passing through.

# Esomeprazole (Nexium)

*Proton Pump Inhibitor (PPI) – Acid Reducer*

When stomach acid climbs too high,
Esomeprazole says goodbye.
A **proton pump inhibitor**, sleek and smart,
It stops the burn before it starts.
It blocks the **$H^+/K^+$ ATPase**,
Deep in gastric lining's maze.
Less acid means less pain and flare—
**GERD**, **ulcers**, and more repair.
Used for **erosive esophagitis**, too,
And **H. pylori** with a triple crew.
Also for **Zollinger-Ellison syndrome**,
Where acid levels wildly roam.
Side effects may still arise:
**Headache**, **nausea**, **diarrhea's** surprise.
**Constipation**, gas, or dry mouth, maybe,
And **low magnesium** if used too daily.
With long-term use, watch the chart—
**B12 deficiency** may start.
Also think of **fracture risk**,
So **bone health** checks should not be brisk.

No black box warning, but take note:

It **may mask cancer** in the throat.

So if symptoms linger, do not stall—

Refer for testing, rule it all.

Drug interactions? Yes, a few:

It may affect what **Clopidogrel** can do.

It lowers how that drug gets turned,

So clot prevention might get burned.

Also affects **pH-dependent drugs**,

Like **ketoconazole**, causing shrugs.

Space out timing, know the flow,

And teach what patients need to know.

Take **before meals**, usually in the morn,

So acid's silenced before it's born.

Swallow whole—don't crush or split,

That enteric coat has purpose in it.

So Nexium, "the purple pill,"

Brings reflux, ulcers, acid to still.

With careful teaching, labs, and care,

It soothes the gut with nurse-aware flair.

# Famotidine (Pepcid)

*H2 Receptor Antagonist – Acid Reducer*

When acid's creeping late at night,
Famotidine helps make it right.
An **H2 blocker**, smooth and fast,
It helps those burning flares not last.
It blocks **histamine at H2**,
In parietal cells—acid's crew.
So less acid flows into place,
Bringing comfort, calm, and space.

Used for **GERD**, **ulcers**, **indigestion**,
And part of ulcer prevention suggestion.
Also used IV in the ICU scene,
To stop stress ulcers from getting mean.
Side effects? Mild for most:
**Headache**, **constipation**, some might post.
**Dizziness**, or **diarrhea**, may arrive,
But generally, patients take it and thrive.

No black box, but use with care
In **renal impairment**—dose with flair.

Too much can bring on CNS daze—
**Confusion**, especially in elder days.
It's safer than some PPI trends,
For short-term use or weekend mends.
But don't forget it **can interact**,
Though less than Cimetidine, in fact.

Teach to take it **once or twice a day**,
With or without food—it's okay.
But don't take with **antacids near**,
Space them out by an hour clear.
Teach signs of **GI bleed**, just in case—
Like black stools or iron taste.
And if chest pain still won't back down,
It may not be reflux that's around.

So Pepcid helps reduce the flame,
When GERD or ulcers play their game.
With simple care and nursing guide,
It brings sweet comfort from inside.

# Ferrous Sulfate (Iron)

*Iron Supplement – Hematinic / Antianemic Agent*

When hemoglobin runs too low,
Ferrous sulfate helps it grow.
An **iron salt** that builds the store,
So oxygen can flow some more.
Used for **iron-deficiency anemia**,
In blood loss, diet gaps, or previa.
Pregnancy, periods, GI bleed—
Wherever iron fills the need.

It helps the body **make red cells**,
So tired hearts can pump like bells.
But it must be **absorbed just right**,
Or constipation joins the fight.
Side effects? Oh, yes—take heed:
**Constipation**, **black stools**, common indeed.
**Nausea**, **cramps**, metallic taste,
So dosing right avoids the waste.

Teach patients **take it on an empty gut**,
But **with food** if cramps are in the cut.

Yet no **milk**, no **antacids near**,
They block absorption—make that clear.
Pair it with **vitamin C**—a friend!
It helps the iron absorb and blend.
Avoid with **calcium, tetracycline,**
And **levothyroxine**, they'll intertwine.

No black box warning, but don't ignore—
In **kids**, it can be fatal if they explore.
**Keep bottles locked and out of sight**,
Iron overdose is no small fight.
Monitor **H&H**, retics, and ferritin,
To make sure that the gains begin.
And teach them not to be alarmed—
**Dark stools** don't mean they've been harmed.

So ferrous sulfate—small, but bold,
Brings energy back and strength to hold.
With teaching firm and follow-through,
This little pill does wonders for you.

# Fidaxomicin (Dificid)

*Macrolide Antibiotic – C. difficile–Specific Agent*

When **C. diff** strikes with foul surprise,
Fidaxomicin's the one that flies.
A **macrolide**, but not so wide—
It targets **Clostridioides** with pride.
It **blocks RNA polymerase**,
So C. diff can't complete its phase.
It stays **in the gut**, not system-wide,
So fewer side effects will ride.

Used for **C. difficile infection (CDI)**,
Especially when recurrence won't comply.
It's **first-line** now in many a case,
Because it works with gentle grace.
Side effects? They're not too grim:
**Nausea, GI pain**, or **bloating limb**.
**Anemia, neutropenia**—rare,
But monitor labs with nursing care.

**No black box warning** on this one,
But cost and access can weigh a ton.

It's pricey, so it's saved for times
When other treatments failed to shine.
Teach to take it **twice a day**,
**10 days straight**, don't miss the way.
With or without food—it's fine,
But consistency is key to align.

Unlike vanco or metronidazole,
It won't disrupt the flora role.
That's why recurrence rates are low,
The **microbiome** gets time to grow.
No big drug interactions known,
But still review the meds they own.
And always teach infection care—
**Handwashing**, **sanitizing**, everywhere.

So Dificid brings targeted might,
When C. diff gives a nasty fight.
A gut-specific, narrow gun—
That stops the spores so healing's won.

# Glycerin Suppositories

*Hyperosmotic Laxative – Rectal Evacuant*

When bowels won't respond to cheer,
Glycerin gets things into gear.
A **hyperosmotic** rectal aid,
To soften stool that's overstayed.
It pulls in water to the site,
Creating pressure, soft and light.
It **stimulates the rectal wall**,
So stubborn poop begins to fall.

Used for **constipation**, gentle and quick,
Safe for **infants**, **pregnant**, or those sick.
Often given when time is tight,
To bring relief without a fight.
Side effects? They're rarely seen—
But **rectal irritation** may convene.
A bit of burning, cramp, or sting,
But nothing long or worrying.

No black box warning—nurses cheer!
It's one of the safest laxatives here.

But still don't overuse each day,
Or bowel tone may fade away.
Teach them how to use it right:
Lie on the side, insert in sight.
Keep it in for **15 minutes max**,
And hold if you can—don't relax too fast.

It works within a gentle span,
**15 to 30 minutes**, give or plan.
No systemic absorption here,
So fewer risks than meds you steer.
No real drug interactions, true,
But teach hygiene and safety, too.
Especially in peds or fragile skin—
Use with care and calm within.

So glycerin slides in with grace,
To help the bowels find their pace.
A gentle push, a nudge, a glide—
That helps the body poop with pride.

# Glycopyrrolate (Robinul)

*Anticholinergic – Antisecretory / Antispasmodic Agent*

When secretions flow too much, too fast,
Glycopyrrolate helps them pass.
An **anticholinergic**, smooth and sly,
It dries things up and calms the GI.
It blocks **acetylcholine's command**,
So **smooth muscles** ease, and dry glands stand.
Used for **ulcers, drooling, IBS pain**,
And pre-op to keep airways plain.
It **reduces saliva**, gastric juice,
And keeps spasms from running loose.
So surgical fields stay nice and dry,
And bowels don't twist or cramp and cry.
Side effects? The usual pair—
**Dry mouth, blurred vision**, and beware:
**Urinary retention, tachycardia** too,
And **constipation** may come through.
Less likely than others to cross the brain,
So **less sedation**, less mental strain.
A great choice when CNS calm
Is needed without the sleepy balm.

No black box warning, but still be wise—
In **glaucoma**, **BPH**, the risks may rise.
Also avoid in **myasthenia gravis** folk,
It can worsen weakness with one poke.
Teach to suck on **ice chips** or gum,
For dry mouth woes that often come.
And watch for **heat stroke**, since this friend
Can block the body's cooling trend.
**Take before meals** if it's for gut,
So the antispasmodic doors can shut.
And teach to report if vision blurs,
Or if they can't pee, as that occurs.
Few drug interactions, but still assess—
Additive effects may cause distress
With **other anticholinergic drugs** around,
The dryness and confusion may compound.
So Robinul dries, calms, and protects,
With careful nursing side-effect checks.
From spasms to secretions, it holds its ground,
Helping patients feel safe and sound.

# Golimumab (Simponi)

*Monoclonal Antibody – TNF-alpha Inhibitor*

When inflammation flares too strong,
And gut attacks go on too long,
Golimumab steps in the fight—
A **TNF-blocker** with targeted might.
It binds to **tumor necrosis factor (TNF)**,
And turns inflammatory storms to rest.
Used for **ulcerative colitis** flare,
And **rheumatoid arthritis**, too, with care.
It calms immune response gone wild,
So healing can begin, not reviled.
A **monoclonal antibody**, sleek and clean,
It keeps that cytokine machine unseen.
Given **subcutaneously** with ease,
Once a month to help disease.
But first, check patients through and through—
Because infection risk runs true.
**Black box warning**—loud and clear:
**Serious infections** may appear.
**TB**, **fungal**, or **bacterial**, fast—
Screen them all before the first blast.

Also watch for **lymphoma**, rare,
And other cancers hiding there.
Especially in children and teens,
That warning lives in black box scenes.
Side effects? Let's take a look:
**Injection site reactions**, in the book.
**Headache, fatigue, hypertension** flares,
And **upper respiratory** stuff shares.
Monitor **CBC** and **LFT**,
And signs of infection—look closely.
Teach to call for **fever**, chills,
Or anything that breaks the stills.
No live vaccines while it's in play,
The immune system's kept at bay.
And don't combine with other TNF-blockers—
That's a recipe for red-flag shockers.
So Simponi, precise and strong,
Calms the gut when things go wrong.
With screening, teaching, and nursing plan,
It helps the healing gently span.

# Hydrocortisone Rectal Foam (Cortifoam)

*Corticosteroid – Anti-inflammatory (Rectal)*

When rectal pain begins to roar,
And swelling knocks on GI's door,
Cortifoam brings a steroid wave—
To calm the flare and symptoms save.
It's **hydrocortisone**, rectal form,
To treat the sites where bowels storm.
Used for **ulcerative colitis** flares,
That settle low in rectal lairs.
It **reduces inflammation** fast,
With local action, effects that last.
It won't absorb as much inside,
So systemic risks often slide.
Side effects? Still may arise:
**Burning, itching, rectal cries**.
Long-term use may thin the skin,
Or cause **bleeding**, if used again and again.
Rarely, **systemic absorption** can sneak,
Causing **adrenal suppression** in the weak.

**Hyperglycemia**, mood swings, too,

So monitor if symptoms accrue.

No black box, but be alert—

Steroid risks can still exert.

Avoid in **rectal infections near**,

Like **fungal**, **TB**, or **viral gear**.

Teach the patient how to dose:

**After a bowel movement** is best, the most.

Shake the can and gently spray,

Hold for a bit—don't rush away.

Limit use to **short-term aid**,

Long-term risks must be weighed.

Report if bleeding comes to stay,

Or if pain gets worse day by day.

Interactions? Minimal, true—

But if using **other steroids**, review.

It may enhance their systemic load,

So monitor down that medication road.

So Cortifoam helps soothe and mend,

When colitis flares without an end.

With nursing care and proper tone,

It brings relief right to the zone.

# Hydrocortisone Suppositories/Cream (Anusol-HC)

*Corticosteroid – Anti-inflammatory / Anti-itch*

When itching, swelling, pain unite,

Hydrocortisone helps make it right.

In **suppository** or **topical cream**,

It soothes the burn and calms the scream.

It's a **steroid**, mild yet strong,

That blocks inflammation gone wrong.

For **hemorrhoids**, **proctitis**, or **anal flare**,

It brings quick comfort right down there.

It blocks the **arachidonic chain**,

So swelling, redness, and pain don't remain.

Used **topically or rectally**, too,

It's versatile in what it can do.

Side effects? Mostly local in place:

**Burning, dryness,** or **skin irritation** face.

With long-term use, risks creep in—

Like **thinning skin** or lightened skin.

**Systemic absorption** is still a chance,

If used too much—or with broken stance.

**Adrenal suppression**, mood swings, face puff,
So short-term use is often enough.
No black box warning, but don't dismiss
The risks if patients over-miss.
Not for **infections** like fungal near—
It can make them worse, not disappear.
Teach patients to wash hands before,
Apply **a thin layer**, nothing more.
For suppositories, lie on side,
Insert gently—let it slide.
Advise to use it **after bowel** move,
That's when the treatment finds its groove.
And **don't use more than prescribed**,
To keep steroid safety vibes alive.
No big interactions known to date,
But monitor use so it won't escalate.
Especially with other steroids in line,
Watch for systemic overlap over time.
So Anusol-HC or Prep H cream,
Deliver relief like a healing dream.
With teaching, timing, and nurse-led grace,
They soothe the burn in a tender place.

# Hyoscyamine (Levsin)

*Anticholinergic / Antispasmodic – GI Smooth Muscle Relaxant*

When spasms twist the gut too tight,
Hyoscyamine sets things right.
A cousin to atropine in its game,
It soothes the bowels and calms the flame.
It **blocks acetylcholine's effect**,
So **GI motility** can disconnect.
Used for **IBS**, **ulcers**, and more,
It slows the gut from end to core.
It also helps with **pancreatitis pain**,
And bladder spasms that constrain.
Even in palliative care,
It dries secretions hanging there.
Side effects? Anticholinergic in style:
**Dry mouth**, **blurred vision**, dizzy awhile.
**Constipation**, **urinary retention**, too,
And **tachycardia** might break through.
Be careful with elders—**CNS fog** may rise,
**Confusion**, **delirium**, not a surprise.
**Heat intolerance** also appears,

Since sweating stops and overheating nears.

No black box warning, but caution still—

Especially if heart or bladder's ill.

Avoid in **glaucoma**, **BPH**, and such,

And those with **myasthenia**—don't touch

Teach to take it **before a meal**,

To let the antispasmodic seal.

And don't chew or crush the tab—

It's made to work as a full rehab.

Watch for **overdose signs** with care:

**Hot, dry skin**, pupils that stare.

**Hallucinations**, fast pulse in the mix—

Call the doc, don't try home tricks.

Interactions? Yes, it may boost

Other **anticholinergics**' use.

Additive effects can quickly snow,

So keep the full med list in tow.

So Levsin brings relief, no doubt,

When GI pain is acting out.

With teaching sharp and nursing wise,

You'll help the gut harmonize.

# Infliximab (Remicade)

*Monoclonal Antibody – TNF-alpha Inhibitor*

When inflammation storms too loud,
And ulcerative flares are fierce and proud,
Infliximab steps in with might—
A **TNF-alpha blocker** that calms the fight.
A **monoclonal antibody** true,
It binds to TNF and subdues the crew.
Used in **Crohn's** and **ulcerative colitis**,
To quiet the gut and tame arthritis.
Also helps in **RA**, **psoriasis**, more—
Where autoimmune rage shakes the core.
But it's **IV only**, slow and planned,
With monitoring close and nurse in hand.
**Black box warning** loud and clear:
**Serious infections** may appear—
**TB**, **fungal**, or sepsis deep,
So **screen before** this med you keep.
Also risk of **lymphoma**, rare,
Especially in teens—so handle with care.
Monitor for signs that linger long—
Fatigue, swollen glands, or something wrong.

Side effects? Let's walk the track:
**Infusion reactions** may attack—
**Fever**, **chest pain**, chills, and rash,
So premeds may prevent the crash.
Watch for **liver injury**, **heart failure signs**,
**Neutropenia**, and autoimmune lines.
Even **delayed reactions** days away,
So educate well—they must not delay.
No live vaccines while it's in play,
The immune system's held at bay.
And teach to call for fever, cough,
Or night sweats they can't shake off.
**Given every 8 weeks** once you start,
After loading doses do their part.
Monitor **CBC**, **LFT**, and more,
And **TB tests** before you pour.
So Remicade's a powerful friend,
When GI wars won't seem to end.
But nurse with care and patient trust,
Because safety first is always a must.

# Ivermectin (Stromectol)

*Antiparasitic Agent – Broad-Spectrum Antihelminthic*

When parasites invade the scene,
Ivermectin comes in clean.
It paralyzes bugs with might,
So worms let go and lose the fight.
It binds to **chloride channels**, you see,
Disrupts their **nervous activity**.
They stop their grip, they lose their place—
And exit fast without a trace.
Used for **strongyloidiasis**, GI bound,
And **onchocerciasis** where it's found.
Also fights **scabies**, **lice**, and such—
A wide-spectrum med, and not too much.
Side effects? Mild for most,
But still some signs we should post:
**Dizziness**, **nausea**, or **rash** may show,
**Pruritus** or **swelling** as bugs let go.
In **high parasite loads**, take care—
A **Mazzotti reaction** may flare.
Fever, tachycardia, lymph nodes rise—
It's not the med, but parasite cries.

No black box warning, but proceed
With **neuro checks**, just to heed.
Rare **CNS effects** can appear—
Especially when dosing isn't clea
**Take on an empty stomach** for best,
So absorption can pass the test.
**One dose** is often all they need,
Though sometimes follow-ups succeed.
It interacts with few, but note—
**Warfarin's effects** may rock the boat.
And though it's safe, still use with care
In those with brain parasite flare.
Pregnancy? Caution's the tone,
Weigh the risks if it's unknown.
Teach them hygiene—clean the space,
To keep reinfection from taking place.
So Stromectol, the parasite foe,
Helps make the GI clean and flow.
With dosing wise and nurse's guide,
It clears the bugs that hide inside.

# Lactobacillus Acidophilus

*Probiotic – GI Flora Restorer*

When gut bugs vanish, wiped away,
Lactobacillus comes to stay.
A **probiotic**, safe and sound,
It helps restore the flora ground.
This friendly bug, found in the gut,
Fights bad bacteria in a rut.
It **lowers pH**, makes acids right,
And crowds out bugs that cause a fight.
Used for **diarrhea, antibiotic strains**,
To ease the gas and soothe the pains.
Helpful in **IBS** or yeast rebirth,
And boosts immunity for what it's worth.
Side effects? They're pretty few—
**Gas, bloating**, maybe a poo or two.
But rarely does it cause much harm,
It's gentle, friendly, full of charm
**No black box warning** on this aid,
But don't assume it's always okay-ed.
In **immunocompromised** or very frail,
There's still a risk, so don't derail.

Teach to take it **daily, same time**,

With or without food—it's fine.

But space it out from **antibiotic meds**,

So both can do their work instead.

Look for **refrigeration** on the label,

Or shelf-stable if it's stable.

It comes in **capsules**, powders, more,

Each with CFUs to restore.

No major drug interactions known,

But check the med list they've been shown.

And remind them: it's **not FDA-approved**

For treating disease—it just improves.

So acidophilus does its part,

To help the gut and give a start.

With nurse's tips and steady pace,

It brings the balance back in place.

# Lactulose (Constulose, Generlac)

*Osmotic Laxative / Ammonia Reducer – Synthetic Disaccharide*

When bowels stall or toxins rise,
Lactulose steps in, kind and wise.
A **sugar that's synthetic-made**,
But oh, the healing path it's laid.
It draws in water—**osmotic pull**,
To make the stools soft, loose, and full.
Used for **chronic constipation** woes,
And **hepatic encephalopathy** shows.
In liver failure, it clears the haze,
By pulling **ammonia** from the maze.
It acidifies the colon zone,
So **ammonia turns to ammonium**, alone.
That form can't cross the gut's tight wall,
So toxins leave instead of stall.
Mental fog begins to clear,
And patients feel their minds appear
Side effects? Yes, they can show:
**Gas**, **bloating**, **diarrhea's** flow.
**Cramps**, **nausea**, not too rare—

So titrate slow with nursing care.

No black box, but **monitor K+**,

As **hypokalemia** may pass by.

Also **hypernatremia** risk—

So labs are part of this med's checklist.

**Take it orally** or **via rectum**,

Depending on how fast you expect 'em.

Teach to measure doses neat,

And watch for dehydration's beat.

**Takes 24–48 hours** for poop,

But **mental status** may change in a swoop.

In liver patients, watch alert—

A clearer mind means lessened hurt.

Interactions? Not a lot,

But give space from other meds they've got.

And **diabetics**, use with care—

It's sugar-based, so be aware.

So Lactulose, sweet in name,

Helps clear the gut and clear the brain.

With thoughtful dosing and nurse insight,

It brings relief and mental light.

# Lansoprazole (Prevacid)

*Proton Pump Inhibitor (PPI) – Acid Reducer*

When acid's high and damage grows,
Lansoprazole helps it close.
A **PPI**, it's built to tame
The acid pumps that fuel the flame.
It blocks the **H⁺/K⁺ ATPase** flow,
In parietal cells where acids go.
Used for **GERD, ulcers, Zollinger's plight**,
And healing **erosions** out of sight.

Part of triple therapy, too—
It helps kill **H. pylori's** crew.
Soothing pain and helping mend
The mucosal lining end to end.
Side effects? Let's take a peek:
**Headache, nausea, diarrhea** sneak.
Long-term risks may come with age—
Like **fractures, B12 loss**, or **magnesium cage**.

**No black box**, but still be wise:
Acid suppression has a price.

Over time, it may increase
The risk for **C. diff**, or bone decrease.
Take it **before meals**, once a day,
To block the pumps before they spray.
**Swallow whole**—don't chew or crush,
Or the special coating turns to mush.

Teach them to report new pain,
**Black stools**, **vomiting**, acid rain.
It may **mask signs of cancer**, true—
So persistent symptoms? Time to view.
Space it from meds needing acid to thrive,
Like **ketoconazole** to stay alive.
And though interactions are not extreme,
**Warfarin** and **digoxin** may need a screen.

So Prevacid works deep and strong,
To help the acid stay where it belongs.
With patient care and teaching clear,
It calms the burn that reappears.

# Ledipasvir/Sofosbuvir (Harvoni)

*Antiviral – Direct-Acting Antiviral (DAA) for Hepatitis C*

When Hep C lingers in the vein,
Harvoni helps to stop the strain.
A **combo drug**, a viral block,
To help the liver beat the clock.
**Ledipasvir** halts replication crew,
By blocking **NS5A**—it's true.
**Sofosbuvir** steps in strong and fast,
Blocks **NS5B** so RNA can't last.
Together they bring cure with pride,
In **genotype 1** and others worldwide.
Used for **chronic Hepatitis C**,
In liver disease and liver-free.
**Once daily**, take it whole,
No food restrictions to control.
But don't miss a dose or change the time—
Resistance forms and that's a climb.
Side effects? Let's take a glance:
**Fatigue**, **headache**, loss of dance.
Sometimes **nausea**, **insomnia**, too,
But serious reactions? Rare and few.

No black box for this precise pair,

But use with care—there's still some flare:

**Bradycardia** risk if **amiodarone** joins,

It slows the heart and disrupts the coins

So **monitor heart rate** if both are used,

And warn of dizziness—don't be confused.

Also screen for **HBV coinfection**,

As **reactivation** needs detection.

Drug interactions? Yes, a few:

**Antacids** lower what it can do.

Space by **4 hours** if needed there,

To help the med absorb with care.

**P-gp inducers** are a no-go—

Like **rifampin**, they steal the show.

And **St. John's Wort**? It should be banned,

It blocks absorption as it's planned.

Monitor **LFTs**, **HCV load**,

To watch the cure rate start to grow.

And teach your patients loud and clear:

Harvoni brings the virus near...

Then silences it—**cure in sight**,

When dosing's done just right each night.

# Linaclotide (Linzess)

*Guanylate Cyclase-C Agonist – IBS-C & Chronic Constipation Agent*

When constipation clogs the way,
Linzess helps to clear the day.
A **GC-C agonist**, small but bold,
That tells the gut to break the hold.
It activates **cyclic GMP**,
To **boost chloride and fluid** in the GI stream.
This softens stool, improves the glide,
And helps the bowels open wide.
Used for **IBS with constipation**,
And **CIC**—chronic evacuation frustration.
It works right in the **small intestine**,
No systemic spread—just local blessin'.
Side effects? A few to track:
**Diarrhea** can bounce right back.
Sometimes severe, so teach the signs—
**Dehydration**, cramps, or dizzy lines.
**Gas**, **bloating**, or belly pain,
But usually mild and short in reign.
No **black box**, but here's the deal:

**Not for kids under 6**, for real.
In animal studies, risk was high—
So keep it far from little's eye.
And **ages 6–17?** Avoid for now,
Until more data shows us how.
Take it **before breakfast**, first thing in day,
On **empty stomach**—that's the way.
Swallow whole—don't crush or split,
Capsule coating must stay lit.
If they can't swallow, there's a hack:
Open and sprinkle—nurse-approved track.
But mix it right and take it fast,
No storing doses meant to last.
It doesn't interact too wide,
But teach hydration on the side.
And if diarrhea gets too wild,
Stop the med—recheck the file.
So Linzess helps the bowels release,
Bringing patients back to peace.
With teaching clear and timing tight,
It gets things moving, smooth and light.

# Liraglutide (Saxenda)

*GLP-1 Receptor Agonist – Appetite Suppressant / Weight Management*

When hunger hits too hard, too loud,
Saxenda helps you thin the crowd.
A **GLP-1 agonist**, smooth and smart,
It tells the brain and gut to part.
It mimics **incretin hormone flow**,
To **slow the stomach's emptying** show.
It signals **satiety up top**,
So cravings fade and meals can stop.
Used for **chronic weight control**,
With **BMI** that takes a toll.
Also used in **diabetes**, true—
Though that's its **Victoza** debut.
Side effects? **Nausea**, yes, indeed,
**Vomiting, diarrhea**, may take the lead.
**Constipation, belching, bloating**, too,
Especially when you're starting new.
**Black box warning**—read it clear:
**Thyroid C-cell tumors** may appear.
**Contraindicated** if family tree

Has **MEN-2** or **thyroid C**.

Teach to **inject it once a day**,

In thigh, arm, or belly way.

Rotate sites to keep skin smooth,

And follow the **titration** groove.

Start low, then raise it slow,

To help those GI symptoms go.

Take **any time**, food or not,

But keep it daily—don't forgot.

Teach signs of **pancreatitis pain**—

Sharp, upper belly that won't wane.

If **gallstones** lurk or **nausea grows**,

Call the doc if anything shows.

It may delay some **oral meds**,

So time them right to clear the dregs.

And monitor **glucose**, weight, and labs,

To see how well it helps or drabs.

So Saxenda, with nurse support,

Can help with weight loss—slow, not short.

With mindful steps and patient guide,

It helps them walk with strength and pride.

# Loperamide (Imodium)

*Antidiarrheal – Peripheral Opioid Receptor Agonist*

When diarrhea's running wild,
Loperamide tames the child.
An **opioid-like** med, but don't be scared—
It **acts in the gut**, not elsewhere shared.
It binds to **mu receptors** down below,
To **slow peristalsis** nice and slow.
This gives the colon time to pull
More water back—stools aren't as full.
Used for **acute diarrhea** quick,
Or **chronic issues** that just won't stick.
Also helps in **IBD control**,
To keep the bowels on a better roll.
Side effects? Just a few:
**Constipation**, **cramps**, maybe **nausea** too.
Rarely, **toxic megacolon** risk
In IBD—so don't go brisk
**Black box warning**—don't misuse:
**High doses** cause deadly news.
**QT prolongation**, **ventricular storms**,
**Torsades**, and death in rarest forms.

That's why **max dose** is 16 mg/day—
And only 8 mg OTC, by the way.
It's **not for kids under 2**,
And shouldn't be used if **fever's** due.
Don't give if there's **bloody stool**,
Or **C. diff suspicion**—that's the rule.
It keeps the bug trapped deep inside,
Which can lead to **sepsis** worldwide.
Teach to **hydrate**, rest the gut,
Use **clear fluids**, nothing but.
And stop if **constipation starts**,
Or pain builds up in lower parts.
**No major drug interactions**,
But caution with **CYP**-based reactions.
And remind them not to chase the dose—
It's not for euphoria, just stool control, close.
So Imodium, when used with care,
Can stop the runs and help repair.
With nurse-led guidance, timing right,
It calms the gut and holds things tight.

# Lubiprostone (Amitiza)

*Chloride Channel Activator – Laxative for IBS-C & CIC*

When stools are stuck and won't come clear,
Lubiprostone draws them near.
A **chloride channel opener** true,
It brings in water to help pass through.
It acts on **ClC-2** in gut's small space,
To **boost fluid** into the place.
That softens stool and starts the flow,
For bowels that just won't go.

Used in **chronic idiopathic constipation**,
And **IBS-C in women's population**.
Also helps in **opioid-induced** distress—
When pain meds cause a poop-less mess.
Side effects? Yup, be aware:
**Nausea**, **diarrhea**, and **gas** may flare.
**Headache**, **bloating**, dizzy spells,
But nothing worse if teaching gels.

No **black box warning**, but still stay wise,
**Dyspnea** can catch them by surprise—

It's usually brief, right after the dose,
But mention it so they don't get close.
Teach to **take with food and water**,
To reduce the nausea it may slaughter.
Capsules should be **swallowed whole**,
No crushing here—it breaks the goal.

Not for use in **bowel block**,
So assess before you start the clock.
And **pregnancy?** Use with care—
Category C, so doc beware.
No major drug-to-drug concern,
But always check so nothing burns.
It works **locally**, not through the vein,
So systemic effects are mostly plain.

So Amitiza brings the flow back fast,
For sluggish guts that hold too fast.
With gentle steps and nursing grace,
It helps the bowels find their pace.

# Magnesium Citrate

*Osmotic Laxative – Bowel Evacuant / Saline Cathartic*

When the bowels need a mighty shove,
Magnesium Citrate gives a push with love.
An **osmotic laxative**, bold and fast,
It pulls in water and clears out the past.
It works by drawing fluid in,
To make the stool both soft and thin.
Used for **constipation** hard to tame,
And **bowel prep** before a scope or game.

**Oral solution**, lemony tart,
Works in hours—so don't depart!
Keep a toilet close in view,
'Cause when it hits, it follows through.
Side effects? Well, just a few:
**Cramping, diarrhea**, rushing you.
**Nausea, bloating**, electrolyte shift—
So monitor labs to catch the drift.

In **renal failure**, hold it back—
**Magnesium buildup** risks attack.

Watch for signs: **weakness**, **low BP**,
**Heart block**, **bradycardia**—seriously.
No black box, but nurse with care,
Especially in those with heart meds there.
**Digoxin**, **diuretics**, ACEs too—
All may worsen what's already due.

Teach to **chill** the bottle before,
And drink it down—don't sip or pour.
Then follow up with **plenty of water**,
To aid the flush and make it softer.
Not for **long-term** use or daily go—
Just now and then, or for the show.
And if there's **blockage**, pain, or bleed,
Magnesium Citrate's not the need.

So for quick relief that clears the gate,
This saline lax works really great.
With nurse instructions in good form,
It clears the gut before the storm.

# Magnesium Hydroxide (Milk of Magnesia)

*Osmotic Laxative / Antacid – Saline Agent*

When bowels stall or acid bites,
Milk of Magnesia sets things right.
A **magnesium-based** gentle tool,
To soothe the burn or move the stool.
It draws in water, softens waste,
And helps the bowels move with haste.
Used for **occasional constipation**,
And **heartburn** in low irritation.

It neutralizes acid fast,
But don't let long-term use just last.
Too much can cause a stool cascade—
**Diarrhea** from the dose you made.
Side effects? **Cramping**, **loose bowels** swell,
And **electrolyte imbalances** as well.
**Hypermagnesemia** is the fear,
Especially when the kidneys aren't clear.

So in **renal patients**, skip this med—
Magnesium can rise and cause deep dread:
**Weakness**, **hypotension**, **heart block**, slow—
Nurses need to watch that flow.
No black box warning, but still alert—
Overuse can quietly hurt.
It's not for **daily** or routine use,
So patient teaching is a must, let loose.

Give **on an empty stomach** for best effect,
And chase with water to protect.
It works in **30 minutes to 6 hours**,
Depending on dose and GI powers.
Don't give with **tetracyclines**, iron, or dig,
As it can bind and block their gig.
Space meds by **2 hours** just to be safe,
So absorption stays in place.

So Milk of Magnesia, white and mild,
Helps things pass when things are piled.
With nurse advice and timing tight,
It brings the gut back into light.

# Mebendazole (Emverm)

*Anthelmintic – Broad-Spectrum Anti-Parasitic*

When worms are squirming deep inside,
Mebendazole stops their ride.
A **broad-spectrum** anti-worming star,
It targets parasites near and far.
It **blocks glucose uptake** on the sly,
So worms go hungry, starve, and die.
Their tubulin gets wrecked as well—
No structure left, no tale to tell.

Used for **pinworms**, **whipworms**, **hook**, and **round**,
It clears the gut where bugs are found.
One dose, then maybe dose again—
To make sure none come back in.
Side effects? They're pretty rare,
But **abdominal pain**, some may share.
**Gas, diarrhea, rash,** or **itch**,
But most folks feel just fine and switch.

In **high doses** or **longer use**,
You might see **liver lab abuse**,

So **LFTs, CBC** need track
If doses go beyond the pack.
**No black box warning**, but use with care,
Especially if infection's rare.
In **pregnancy**, it's best to wait—
Risk in early term isn't great.

Teach to **take with food**, not bare,
It boosts absorption then and there.
And **treat the whole household**, too,
Because worms can spread like colds do.
Wash all linens, clean with pride—
These bugs can linger, sneak, and hide.
And teach good hand hygiene each day,
To keep the eggs from making way.

So Emverm stands, a trusted tool,
To rid the gut of parasites cruel.
With patient teaching, clean and true,
The bugs are gone—and health breaks through.

# Mesalamine (Asacol, Pentasa, Lialda)

*Aminosalicylate – Anti-inflammatory for IBD*

When colitis starts to rage and swell,
Mesalamine helps break the spell.
An **aminosalicylate** in disguise,
That calms the gut and quiets the cries.
It works by blocking **prostaglandin flow**,
Reducing **inflammation** down below.
Used in **ulcerative colitis** most,
And sometimes **Crohn's**, from coast to coast.
Comes in **oral, rectal foam, or suppository**,
To meet the flare with local glory.
From **mouth to rectum**, brands vary wide—
Like **Pentasa** through the GI slide.
Side effects? Let's take a glance:
**Headache**, **nausea**, cramps by chance.
**Flatulence**, rash, and rare **fever**,
And **nephrotoxicity** in a small receiver.
So check **renal labs** from the start—
**BUN, creatinine** play their part.

Rarely, **pancreatitis** may ignite,

Or **blood disorders** come to light.

No black box warning, but here's the deal:

Use caution if the **kidneys squeal**.

Also watch for **sulfa confusion**,

(Sulfasalazine's the one with fusion).

Teach to take it **same time daily**,

Don't crush or chew—it's released strategically.

Some forms **with food**, some without—

So follow the label, there's no doubt.

Interactions? Just a few:

May reduce **digoxin's** bio-view.

And additive effects may rise

With **NSAIDs**, causing renal surprise.

So Mesalamine calms the flame,

When IBD plays its painful game.

With nurse instruction, labs in tow,

It helps the gut begin to glow.

# Mesalamine Rectal (Canasa, Rowasa)

*Aminosalicylate – Local Anti-inflammatory for IBD*

When rectal flares ignite with pain,
Mesalamine steps in again.
But this time, it's a **local spray**—
**Suppository** or **enema** saves the day.
**Canasa** comes in bullet form,
To soothe the rectum when it's warm.
**Rowasa** flows in enema style,
To coat the **sigmoid** and lower mile.
It blocks **prostaglandin pathways** deep,
So inflammation starts to sleep.
For **ulcerative colitis**, mild and low,
It helps the bleeding, cramps, and flow.
Side effects? A few to name:
**Rectal discomfort**, burning flame.
**Gas**, **cramping**, or urgency,
But most still feel relief, you see.
Rare but real: **allergic signs**,
**Rash**, **fever**, or **blood in lines**.

Even **pancreatitis** may show,
So teach your patients what to know.
**No black box warning**, still take care—
Monitor if symptoms flare.
Not for use in **renal decline**,
So check **creatinine** over time.
Teach to **retain it overnight**,
Or at least for one full hour's fight.
Suppositories melt and spread with ease,
While enemas should be held to please.
Use **before bed**—that's the goal,
To let it work while on patrol.
And warn of stains on sheets or clothes—
The fluid leaks if not well-posed.
Don't confuse it with oral brands—
This one works with local hands.
And teach to **shake the bottle well**,
So Rowasa's magic doesn't quell.
So Mesalamine, rectal form,
Brings the lower gut back to norm.
With patient trust and nurse-led guide,
It heals the flare from deep inside.

# Metoclopramide (Reglan)

*Prokinetic / Antiemetic – Dopamine Antagonist*

When the stomach's slow and won't let go,
Metoclopramide helps it flow.
A **dopamine blocker**, swift and neat,
It helps the GI tract compete.
It **increases gastric motility**,
And **tightens LES activity**.
So food moves forward, not around—
Reducing **GERD** and **nausea** sound.
Used for **gastroparesis**, nausea's curse,
**Post-op vomiting**, or chemo worse.
Sometimes used to help **tube feeds** pass,
And **migraine nausea** fade at last.
Side effects? Oh yes, take heed:
**Drowsiness**, **restlessness**, maybe **speed**.
**Diarrhea**, **fatigue**, or dizzy feel,
But there's a darker part to reveal
**Black box warning** stands out strong:
**Tardive dyskinesia** if used too long.
**Involuntary movements**, face or hand—
So short-term use is what we plan.

Also watch for **EPS signs**:

**Dystonia**, **tremors**, awkward lines.

More common in the elderly crew,

And women may see symptoms too.

**Depression, suicidal thoughts,**

May appear in vulnerable spots.

So mental health should not be missed—

Ask how they feel, it's on the list.

Teach to take it **30 minutes pre-meal,**

And **at bedtime** for motility deal.

IV, IM, or by mouth it comes,

But the oral route is used by tons.

Interactions? Yes—**CNS depressants,**

And **antipsychotics**, strong contestants.

**Levodopa** is a no-go pair,

Their actions cancel in the air.

So Reglan helps the gut move fast,

But shouldn't be a med that lasts.

With nurse instructions, screening tight,

It gets things going when they're not right.

# Metronidazole (Flagyl)

*Antibiotic / Antiprotozoal – Anaerobic & GI Infection Fighter*

When gut infections start to swell,
Metronidazole fights them well.
A **nitroimidazole** brave and bold,
It stops the bugs in dark strongholds.
It **disrupts DNA** from deep inside,
So anaerobes can't grow or hide.
Used for **C. diff**, **diverticulitis**, **H. pylori** blends,
And **intra-abdominal abscess** ends.
Also treats **giardiasis**, **trich**, and more,
Even **bacterial vaginosis** lore.
But GI bugs are its main fame,
Where **anaerobic pathogens** stake claim.
Side effects? Let's take a look:
**Nausea**, **metallic taste**, they book.
**Headache**, **cramps**, and **appetite drop**,
**Urine turns dark**—don't call the doc.
But there's a big one, loud and clear:
**NO alcohol** while it's near.
A **disulfiram-like reaction** strikes—
With **flushing**, **vomit**, headache spikes.

**Black box warning** must be known:
**Carcinogenic risk** in rodent zones.
So long-term use? Not advised—
Only when the benefit's prized.
Teach to take it **with some food**,
To calm the stomach-mood.
**Complete the course**, don't miss a day,
Even if they feel okay.
Drug interactions, there are a few:
**Warfarin**'s effect is raised in you.
And **lithium, phenytoin, phenobarb**
May need adjusting on the chart.
In **pregnancy**, avoid **first trimester**,
Unless the risk is truly festered.
But second and third? It may proceed—
If treating a strong enough need.
So Flagyl fights the bugs below,
Where oxygen fears to go.
With nursing care and teaching tight,
It helps the gut return to right.

# Misoprostol (Cytotec)

*Prostaglandin Analog – Ulcer Prevention / Cervical Ripening Agent*

When NSAIDs harm the stomach lining,
Misoprostol keeps it shining.
A **prostaglandin analog**, it's true—
It helps the gut protect its glue.
It boosts **mucus and bicarbonate**,
To coat the walls and regulate.
Reduces acid, heals the sore,
And guards against **ulcers** evermore.

Used for **NSAID-induced ulcer prevention**,
It lowers bleeding risk and tension.
But it's also used in OB land,
To help the cervix ripen as planned.
Side effects? Be aware:
**Diarrhea**, **cramps**, and **nausea** flair.
**Abdominal pain**, **gas**, and chills,
It can cause some GI spills.

**Black box warning**, bold and loud:

**Pregnancy use is not allowed** (for GI use).

It causes **uterine contractions** fast,

Which may lead to **miscarriage** if it's passed.

So always **ask about pregnancy state**,

Before you dispense or educate.

And **contraception** is a must,

While on this med, in full nurse trust.

Teach to **take with meals**, no rush,

To reduce cramping and the flush.

And don't double if a dose is gone—

Resume next one and carry on.

Interactions? Not too wide,

But caution with **oxytocics** side.

When used for OB induction, know

That combos may increase uterine flow.

So Cytotec has double fame—

For ulcers or the birth-time game.

With nurse-led screening and deep insight,

It protects the gut or starts birth right.

# Neomycin

*Aminoglycoside Antibiotic – Bowel Prep / Ammonia Reducer*

When gut bacteria must be cleared,
Neomycin is the med that's steered.
An **aminoglycoside** that's strong and fast,
But **not absorbed**—it stays and lasts.
It **binds the 30S ribosomal crew**,
So proteins can't be built anew.
Used to **sterilize the bowel** clean
Before GI surgery steps on scene.
Also helps in **hepatic states**,
Like **encephalopathy** that frustrates.
It reduces **ammonia-forming bugs**,
So fewer toxins hit brain plugs.
Side effects? Yes, though it's local:
Still may cause a GI focal—
**Nausea**, **bloating**, **cramps**, or **gas**,
But rarely does it fully harass.
Systemic risks are **rare but real**
If gut's integrity starts to peel:
Then **ototoxicity** may rise, With **hearing loss** or dizzy skies.

**Nephrotoxicity** is on the list,
So monitor kidneys if you insist.
Especially if on **other nephrotoxic meds**,
Like **loop diuretics**, that push the dregs.
No **black box** for oral way,
But **parenteral neomycin** says:
**Hearing loss, kidney injury**,
So use it short and carefully.
Teach to take it **exact as told**,
No skipping doses, no freestyle bold.
Used **short-term**, 1–2 days,
Before surgery clears the maze.
In **hepatic encephalopathy**,
It lowers ammonia symptom-free.
But **rifaximin** is now preferred—
Neomycin's use is less observed.
So this gut-focused aminoglycoside,
Is strong, effective, yet needs to hide
Behind short terms and nurse-led checks,
To guard the gut without the wrecks.

# Nitroglycerin Rectal (Rectiv)

Used for **anal fissures**, painful and raw,
**Nitroglycerin rectal** helps soothe the flaw.
A **vasodilator**, smooths the tone,
Relaxes muscles where pain has grown.

**Increases blood flow** to the tear,
Promotes **healing** down there with care.
Apply a **small dose** using a glove,
Insert with caution—no push or shove.

Watch for **headache**, it's very common,
A **drop in BP** may come on sudden.
**Dizziness**, too, may follow fast—
Tell them to **sit** and let it pass.

Avoid with **hypotension** or meds that dilate,
Like **Viagra**—they potentiate.
Use with care in **cardiac conditions**,
Monitor closely with clear premonitions.

Teach to **wash hands** after use,

And not to touch eyes—that's no excuse.

Dose is usually **twice per day**,

As fissures heal, the pain may stray.

# Nizatidine (Axid)

**Nizatidine** works to reduce the **burn**,
A **H2 blocker**—acid's turn.
It lowers **gastric secretions** fast,
For **ulcers**, **GERD**, and pain that lasts.

Take it **once or twice a day**,
With or without food—it's okay.
Give **before meals** or at **bedtime**,
To keep that acid in decline.

Watch for **headache, diarrhea, or rash**,
And **CNS changes**—though those are brash.
Use caution in **renal disease**,
Lower the dose to keep things at ease.

Avoid **antacids** too close in time,
They'll block absorption—cross the line.
Tell patients to **limit smoking and spice**,
Both reduce how well it fights.

Helps heal the gut, reduce the pain,

But monitor if symptoms remain.

It's less used now, but still in play—

Know this drug for NCLEX day.

# Obeticholic Acid (Ocaliva)

**Ocaliva** treats the **bile flow slow**,
For **primary biliary cholangio**.
It works on **FXR receptors** inside,
To **reduce bile acids** liver-wide.

Used in adults with liver strain,
To slow disease and lessen pain.
May be used **alone or with ursodiol**,
But not for those with **liver failure's toll**.

**Pruritus** is the most common woe,
That itchy skin may steal the show.
Also watch for **fatigue, abdominal pain**,
And **increased cholesterol** in the vein.

Monitor **liver function tests**,
AST, ALT—know the rest.
In **cirrhosis**, dosing's key—
**Adjust or hold** if labs go free.

Take **with or without** food or drink,

But don't assume—it's safe to think.

Educate to **report dark urine or yellow eyes,**

Signs the **liver's in distress or compromise.**

# Omeprazole (Prilosec)

**Omeprazole** is a **PPI**,
It shuts the **acid pumps** down dry.
Used for **ulcers**, **GERD**, and healing fast,
It helps the damage from acid pass.

Take it **before meals**, once a day,
**Swallow whole**, no crush or play.
Works best when taken on time,
Not as needed—this ain't a "PRN" line.

**Headache, nausea, abdominal pain**,
Are side effects you might explain.
But long-term use brings deeper risk—
**Bone loss, low magnesium** on the list.

Can lower **B12** if taken too long,
So monitor if something feels wrong.
Increases risk for **C. diff colitis**,
Report new diarrhea—it might invite this.

Avoid with **clopidogrel** if you can,

It blocks the action in that plan.

Teach to avoid **alcohol, smoking, and spice**,

Those make reflux worse—never nice.

# Ondansetron (Zofran)

**Ondansetron** blocks **serotonin's sway**,
To keep the **nausea and vomiting** away.
Used for **chemo**, **surgery**, **GI distress**,
It helps calm the gut and ease the mess.

Acts on the **CNS and GI tract**,
It's fast and strong—that's just a fact.
Give **IV**, **IM**, or **oral, ODT**,
Let it dissolve—it's nausea-free.

**Headache** and **constipation** top the list,
With **QT prolongation** not to miss.
So get that **EKG baseline** down,
Especially with other meds around.

**Monitor electrolytes**, keep them tight—
Low **K+** or **Mg++** can worsen the fight.
Watch for signs of **serotonin syndrome**, too,
Agitation, tremor—report if true.

Safe in peds but **dose with care**,

Age and weight must guide you there.

And always **assess before you give**,

Some nausea's cause is not so "lived."

# Orlistat (Xenical, Alli)

**Orlistat** blocks the **fat you eat**,
It stops the enzymes that help complete.
A **lipase inhibitor**—that's its game,
So **fat's excreted**, not fair game.

Used for **obesity** in adults and teens,
With **diet and exercise** in the means.
Available as **prescription or OTC**,
But **Xenical's stronger**—more potency.

Main side effects? They're GI,
**Oily stools, gas**, and the urge to fly.
**Diarrhea, leaks**, and **frequent trips**,
Warn your patients—no surprise slips.

Take **three times daily with meals**,
Skip the dose if it's low-fat deals.
May impair the **vitamin ADEK**,
So **supplements daily** are the way.

Use caution in **malabsorption** states,

Or with **cholestasis**—not great mates.

Check **liver enzymes** if symptoms grow—

Like dark urine or yellow glow.

# Pancrelipase (Creon, Zenpep, Pancrease)

*Pancreatic Enzyme Replacement – Digestive Aid for Pancreatic Insufficiency*

When the pancreas takes a rest,
Pancrelipase helps digest.
A **mix of enzymes**—lipase, amylase, protease—
It breaks down food in all the ways.
Used in **pancreatic insufficiency**,
Like **CF**, **chronic pancreatitis**, and surgery.
It helps absorb the fats and more,
So patients don't lose weight and store.
It aids in meals and snacktime too,
So nutrients get their passage through.
With **every bite**, it does its part—
Supporting gut and healing start.
Side effects? Let's start mild:
**Bloating**, **gas**, or belly wild.
But **high doses** raise concern—
**Fibrosing colonopathy** can return.
**No black box**, but heed this rule:
Don't exceed the enzyme pool.

Especially in kids with CF care—
Too much can harm the colon there.
Teach to take it **with meals, not late**,
And **don't chew or crush**—that seals their fate.
Capsules can be opened, sprinkled soft
On **acidic food**—like applesauce, oft.
Avoid **alkaline foods** with the bead,
They'll break the enzymes that you need.
Then follow up with food or drink,
So enzymes mix and don't just sink.
**Hydration** is a must to keep,
And monitor **weight** so gains can creep.
Check for signs of **steatorrhea** still—
That means the dose needs a skillful fill.
Minimal interactions in the med scene,
But always check what's in between.
And remind them it won't replace
Pancreas healing—but helps the race.
So Pancrelipase lends a hand,
To help digestion as it's planned.
With nurse-led care and timing true,
It gives the gut a better view.

# Pantoprazole (Protonix)

*Proton Pump Inhibitor (PPI) – Acid Reducer*

When acid creeps and starts to rise,
Pantoprazole helps neutralize.
A **PPI**, it's strong and sleek,
To quiet reflux flare and peak.
It blocks the **H⁺/K⁺ ATPase** pump,
So acid drops with just one jump.
Used for **GERD**, **erosions**, and **ulcers**, too,
And **Zollinger-Ellison syndrome**, through and through.
Comes **oral or IV**, as needed most,
In hospital care or home-time dose.
Take it **before meals**, not on the fly,
So it can stop the acid supply.
Side effects? Mild, but there:
**Headache**, **nausea**, **diarrhea**, flair.
**B12 deficiency** long-term stays,
And **hypomagnesemia** in rare displays.
No black box, but still beware—
**C. diff infections** may appear.
**Bone fractures** in those who age,
So monitor calcium on that stage.

Don't crush the pill or split in half,

It's enteric-coated on its path.

**Delayed release**, it must unfold

Inside the stomach's secret hold.

Interactions? A few to know:

It may affect drugs that **need low pH to go**.

Like **ketoconazole**, **iron**, and more—

Absorption may not hit the floor.

May also **weaken clopidogrel**,

So heart meds might not work as well.

Still, it's often used with grace,

When GERD or ulcers show their face.

Teach to take it **same time each day**,

And not just when symptoms play.

It's a **preventive**, not a fix-it-quick,

So stay on schedule, that's the trick.

So Protonix brings calm to flame,

When acid tries to stake its claim.

With nursing tips and patient trust,

It soothes the burn—safe, strong, and just.

# Peppermint Oil Capsules (IBgard)

*Antispasmodic / Herbal GI Support – IBS Symptom Relief*

When bowels cramp and twist with flair,
Peppermint oil brings fresh air.
In capsules like **IBgard** form,
It calms the gut and soothes the storm.
It **relaxes smooth muscle tone**,
Especially in the **colon zone**.
A **calcium channel blocker**, light,
That helps reduce the pain and fight.

Used for **IBS**, both C and D,
To ease the gas and urgency.
It tames the bloat, reduces spasm,
And may restore some gut-time chasm.
Side effects? They're mostly chill:
**Heartburn**, burps with minty thrill.
**Dry mouth**, or **nausea** now and then—
But rare are reactions beyond that pen.

No black box warning—herbal grace—
But still, it needs a proper place.

Capsules are **enteric-coated**, bold,
So they don't dissolve till gut takes hold.
Teach to **take on an empty gut**,
30-90 minutes pre-food cut.
Don't chew or crush—just swallow whole,
To get that slow-release control.

Avoid in those with **GERD** or **reflux pain**,
It may make those symptoms remain.
And in **gallbladder disease**, take care—
Peppermint can increase bile's flare.
No known interactions steal the show,
But still review all meds they know.
And teach this isn't meant to cure—
It helps the **symptoms**, not the root for sure.

So peppermint oil, calm and clear,
Brings gentle peace when bowels sneer.
With nursing guide and patient plan,
It soothes the gut just as it can.

# Phenylephrine Rectal (Preparation H)

*Vasoconstrictor – Hemorrhoid Relief / Decongestant*

When swelling strikes and veins protrude,
Phenylephrine comes to soothe.
In **Preparation H**, it holds its ground,
To **shrink the vessels** that are round.
It's a **vasoconstrictor**, alpha-1 strong,
Reducing **blood flow** where it's gone wrong.
It eases **itching, burning, swelling** pain—
And brings relief near the anal vein.

Used for **hemorrhoids**, both inside and out,
It calms the flare, reduces doubt.
Can come in **cream, gel, ointment**, or **supp**,
Applied with care when symptoms erupt.
Side effects? Not too intense:
**Local irritation** makes the most sense.
Rarely, **nervousness** or **BP rise**,
If too much absorbs or dosing's unwise.

No black box, but here's the deal:

Avoid in **HTN** if the dose isn't ideal.

**Heart disease**, **diabetes**, or **thyroid storm**—

Use with caution, not just norm.

Teach to cleanse the area clean,

Before applying this soothing sheen.

Use **after bowel movements**, dry and neat,

And **wash hands** after—don't repeat.

Don't use for more than **seven days**,

Without a provider's guiding gaze.

And watch for bleeding, pain that grows—

Could mean something more than hemorrhoid woes.

Few drug interactions here,

But still, review the list with care.

And no internal forms should be

Used if rectal bleeding's free.

So phenylephrine brings some peace,

When hemorrhoid symptoms won't release.

With gentle care and patient trust,

It helps the flare without a fuss.

# Plecanatide (Trulance)

*Guanylate Cyclase-C Agonist – Laxative for IBS-C & CIC*

When bowels back up, slow and tight,
Plecanatide helps make things right.
A **GC-C agonist**, nice and neat,
It calls for water to join the seat.
It **mimics uroguanylin's tone**,
Working in the **small intestine zone**.
It boosts **chloride and bicarb flow**,
So fluids move and stools can go.
Used for **IBS-C** with bloat and pain,
And **chronic constipation**, hard to tame.
It softens stool and soothes the gut,
With less cramping, strain, or butt.
Side effects? Just a few:
**Diarrhea** is the main one to view.
Rarely, **dizziness** or bloating sneak,
So teach to start when life's not peak.
 **Not for kids under six**, no way—
**Severe dehydration** can make them pay.
In **ages 6 to 17**, no data to trust,
So avoid unless truly a must.

Take it **once a day**, same time roll,

With or without food—it plays both roles.

**Swallow whole**, don't crush or break,

Or the coating won't do what it's meant to make.

If they can't swallow, there's a tip:

**Crush and mix with applesauce**, then sip.

But **take it right away**, not saved—

The mix must go before it's waived.

No black box, but stay alert

If watery stool or cramps hurt.

And **pregnancy risk is low**, they say,

But always check before OK.

Few interactions on the list,

But always check so none are missed.

It works **locally**, not system-wide,

So side effects tend to stay inside.

So Trulance brings the gut some grace,

Restores the flow and clears the space.

With nurse-led teaching, soft and wise,

It gives the bowels peaceful skies.

# Polyethylene Glycol (MiraLAX)

*Osmotic Laxative – Bowel Evacuant / Constipation Relief*

When bowels stall and won't let go,
MiraLAX helps start the flow.
A gentle **osmotic laxative**, clear,
It draws in water, far and near.
It softens stool and makes it glide,
Without the cramps some meds can hide.
Used for **occasional constipation** grace,
Or **bowel prep** in higher-dose case.

It's **tasteless**, **odorless**, easy to blend,
With water, juice, or tea to send.
Dissolves in liquid, once a day,
Takes **1 to 3 days** to clear the way.
Side effects? Mostly light:
**Bloating**, **gas**, or stool that's white.
Rarely **nausea** or **electrolyte shift**,
But it's still one of the smoothest gifts.

No **black box warning**, no big scare,
But hydration helps it work with care.

**Not absorbed**, so side effects are few,

And it's safe for pregnant patients, too.

Teach them not to **double dose**,

More isn't faster—just more gross.

And don't take longer than **a week**,

Unless a doctor clears the streak.

No known drug interactions bad,

But still review all meds they've had.

Safe in **pediatrics** and in age,

A gentle helper on the bowel stage.

So MiraLAX, smooth and clean,

Keeps digestion calm and routine.

With nurse advice and timing right,

It helps the bowels feel more light.

# Prochlorperazine (Compazine)

*Antiemetic / Antipsychotic – Dopamine Antagonist*

When nausea climbs and won't back down,
Prochlorperazine calms the frown.
A **dopamine blocker**, D2's the key,
It quiets nausea, instantly.
Used for **severe nausea and vomiting**, too,
From **chemo**, **migraine**, or **post-op flu**.
It's also used in **psychotic spells**,
But in GI care, it works quite well
It works on the **CTZ in the brain**,
To stop the urge to puke again.
It also acts on inner ear cues,
To settle motion sickness blues.
Side effects? Here's what may come:
**Drowsiness**, **dry mouth**, **dizzy** some.
But the ones to flag with care:
**EPS** can soon be there—
**Tremors**, **rigidity**, **restless leg**,
Or **dystonia** that makes them beg.
And with long use, what may arise?
**Tardive dyskinesia**—jerky surprise.

**Black box warning**, don't ignore:
In **dementia psychosis**, death knocks the door.
So don't use for behavior swings
In older folks with memory things.
Teach to **report strange movements fast**,
Like lip-smacking or blinks that last.
Watch for **sedation, BP low**,
And rise up slowly—let blood flow.
Available **oral, IM, IV**,
Or **suppository** if needed to try.
Dose depends on route and need—
Start low and monitor how they proceed.
Interactions? Yes, beware—
With **CNS depressants**, take care.
**Alcohol**, **opioids**, **benzos** too,
Can make the sedation really stew.
So Compazine, when used just right,
Can bring relief and calm the fight.
With nurse instruction, side effect watch,
It helps the gut without a botch.

# Promethazine (Phenergan)

*Antiemetic / Antihistamine – Phenothiazine Derivative*

When nausea hits with dizzy sway,
Promethazine can save the day.
A **first-gen antihistamine** blend,
With **dopamine-blocking** power to lend.
It works in the **CTZ of the brain**,
To shut down vomit's reflex train.
Also calms **motion sickness, allergy signs**,
And helps with **sedation** at bedtime times
Used for **nausea, vomiting, pre-op dread**,
**Allergies**, or helping someone rest in bed.
Given **oral, rectal, IM, or IV**,
But **IV must be slow** and carefully.
**Black box warning**, very real:
**Severe tissue damage** may steal
The limb if **IV's pushed too fast**,
**Gangrene** can follow—and it's vast.
Also **respiratory depression** risk
In **kids under two**—it's not worth the whisk.
So age matters here—strict and true,
Always check before you do.

Side effects? A familiar stack:

**Drowsiness**, **dizziness**, dry mouth attack.

**Blurred vision**, **hypotension**, woozy might,

And **confusion** in elderly, especially at night.

EPS? It's rare, but there—

**Tremors**, **rigidity**, unblinking stare.

Anticholinergic warnings, too:

**Constipation**, dry mouth coming through.

Teach to avoid **alcohol**,

Or other meds that make them fall.

**Rise slowly**, no sudden race,

To prevent the faint-and-crash embrace.

And remind them it's not for **every** quease—

It's strong and sedating, not just a breeze.

Use **short-term**, not every day,

Unless the doc clears that way.

So Phenergan, in skilled nurse hands,

Can calm the gut and meet demands.

With proper dosing, safe and tight,

It brings the queasy back to right.

# Prucalopride (Motegrity)

*Selective 5-HT4 Receptor Agonist – Prokinetic for Chronic Constipation*

When bowels stall and time runs long,
Prucalopride helps move things along.
It's **Motegrity**, a newer face,
To bring the gut back into pace.
It works on **5-HT4** with grace,
A **serotonin receptor** in the bowel space.
It **stimulates peristalsis**, smooth and bold,
So chronic constipation loses hold.

Used for **CIC** (chronic and slow),
When diet, fiber, and water won't flow.
It's **once a day**, at any hour,
With or without a mealtime power.
Side effects? Let's review:
**Headache, nausea**, maybe a poo too few.
**Diarrhea, abdominal pain**,
And **dizziness** may join the train.

**Watch for mood**—this part is key:

**Suicidal thoughts** have been reported, you see.
So screen for **mental health** before the start,
And follow up with open heart.
**No black box warning**, but still take care,
Especially in those who've had despair.
And **don't use** with **bowel rupture** risk,
Or **Crohn's**, **UC**, or GI twist.

Minimal interactions in the mix,
But check for **other prokinetic tricks**.
And **renal dosing** matters too,
If kidneys slow, adjust what's due.
Teach them results aren't always fast—
It may take **a few days** to move at last.
But when it works, it's steady and strong,
Restoring rhythm that's been gone too long.

So Prucalopride, smooth and bright,
Gives constipated guts new light.
With daily care and patient guide,
It helps the bowels turn the tide.

# Psyllium Fiber (Metamucil)

*Bulk-Forming Laxative – Soluble Fiber Supplement*

When bowels stall or run too fast,
Psyllium helps restore the past.
As **Metamucil**, soft and sweet,
It brings the gut back to its beat.
It's **soluble fiber**, thick and pure,
That bulks the stool and helps it cure.
Used for **constipation**, mild and slow,
And even helps **diarrhea** go.
Also lowers **cholesterol**,
And aids in **glucose** rise control.
With daily use, it helps maintain
A smoother, steadier bowel train.
It absorbs water, forms a gel,
That gives the stool its bulky shell.
But it needs **hydration** to expand—
Or it may block instead of land.
Side effects? Not too wild:
**Gas**, **bloating**, or cramps mild.
But without fluids? That's the key—
You'll risk **impaction**, painfully.

No black box warning on the scene,
But don't forget to keep it clean:
Avoid in **bowel obstruction signs**,
Or strictures where it can't align.
Teach to **mix with 8 oz of fluid**,
And drink it fast—don't let time ruin it.
Don't take it dry—it thickens quick,
Like gut-safe glue that starts to stick.
Can affect absorption, it's true,
So **space other meds by an hour or two**.
And remind them fiber's not a fix—
It's part of daily lifestyle mix.

Safe in **pregnancy, long-term**, too,
As long as water follows through.
And pair with **diet, movement**, grace,
To keep the bowels in a better place.
So psyllium stands, a gut's good friend,
From constipation to the other end.
With nurse support and fiber pride,
It keeps digestion smooth inside.

# Rifaximin (Xifaxan)

*Rifamycin Antibiotic – Non-Absorbed GI Infection Fighter*

When gut bugs bloom where they don't belong,
Rifaximin comes on strong.
A **rifamycin-based** med, precise,
It stays in the gut—doesn't travel twice.
It blocks **bacterial RNA**,
So growth and spread are kept at bay.
Used for **traveler's diarrhea**, quick,
And **IBS-D** when stools are slick.

Also used in **hepatic brains**,
To lower **ammonia's toxic strains**.
Prevents **encephalopathy** flare,
By clearing gut bugs hiding there.
It's **poorly absorbed**, which is the win—
It stays where all the bugs have been.
Less systemic risk, more GI punch,
It clears the trouble after lunch.

Side effects? Not many shown:
**Nausea**, **bloating**, gas alone.

**Headache**, maybe **increased ALT**,

But most folks tolerate it easily.

No **black box warning**, but still take care,

If **C. diff symptoms** linger there.

And teach patients not to share—

It's **antibiotic stewardship** we swear.

Take it **with or without food**,

The dosing depends on what is pursued:

— For **traveler's diarrhea**: three times a day,

— For **IBS-D**: once daily's the way.

— For **hepatic use**: twice a day flow,

Seven to fourteen days, then go.

Interactions? Pretty few—

But always check what else they do.

And don't forget to **finish the pack**,

Even if gut bugs don't come back.

So Xifaxan stays in GI zone,

Fighting bugs where they have grown.

With nurse-led teaching and safe routine,

It clears the gut—and keeps it clean.

# Saccharomyces boulardii (Florastor)

*Probiotic Yeast – Gut Flora Restorer / Antidiarrheal Support*

When gut bugs flee from meds or stress,
Florastor helps to clean the mess.
A **probiotic yeast**, not just a name,
It helps restore the flora game.
It's **Saccharomyces boulardii**,
A gentle yeast that works with glee.
Unlike bacteria, it stands strong
Against **antibiotics** all day long.
Used for **C. diff prevention**, too,
And **traveler's diarrhea** passing through.
Also aids in **IBS flare**,
And post-antibiotic repair.
It **blocks pathogens**, **binds toxins**, fights,
And boosts **IgA** immune delights.
Helps reduce **inflammation**, pain,
While good bacteria rise again.
Side effects? They're rarely seen—
**Gas** or **bloating**, nothing mean.

But in **severely immunocompromised**,
Use with caution—it's not advised.
No black box warning, but
Watch for **fungemia** if lines are cut.
IV lines and **critically ill**?
Skip this yeast—it can cause a chill.
Teach to take it **twice a day**,
With food or not—it's okay.
**Capsule or powder**, both are fine,
And stable at **room temp** over time.
Few interactions, but still be wise—
Always scan with nurse-trained eyes.
And remind them: this isn't cure,
But helps the gut feel more secure.
So Florastor brings balance back,
When antibiotics launch attack.
With patient trust and nurse-led care,
It keeps the gut from wear and tear.

# Scopolamine Patch (Transderm-Scop)

*Anticholinergic – Motion Sickness / Nausea Prevention*

When travel turns the stomach wild,
Scopolamine keeps it mild.
A patch that sits behind the ear,
To keep you steady, calm, and clear.
It blocks **acetylcholine's sway**,
In the **vestibular tract** along the way.
Prevents the signal to the brain
That triggers nausea, motion pain.
Used for **motion sickness**, best of all,
And **post-op nausea** in recovery hall.
It's applied **4 hours before the trip**,
And works for **3 days** on one slip.
Side effects? They sure can show:
**Dry mouth, drowsy, blurred visual flow.**
**Dizziness, urine retention**, too—
That's anticholinergic through and through.
No black box warning here,
But don't use if **glaucoma's near**.

**Angle-closure type** is key—
This patch can spike IOP.
Teach to **wash hands after apply**,
If it gets in the eyes, pupils dilate wide.
And **rotate sites** with each new dose,
To prevent skin issues or overdose.
Remove the patch after **3-day span**,
If needed again, place per plan.
Don't cut or split—just use whole,
So steady dosing stays the goal.
Avoid with **alcohol, CNS meds**,
They all increase sedation heads.
And teach them it may take a bit—
So don't wait 'til motion makes them sit.
So Transderm-Scop, discreet and sleek,
Prevents the nausea motion seeks.
With nurse instruction placed just right,
It keeps the queasy out of sight.

# Semaglutide (Wegovy)

*GLP-1 Receptor Agonist – Weight Management & Appetite Control*

When hunger hits and won't let go,
Semaglutide helps it slow.
As **Wegovy**, it's approved for weight,
To help reduce and regulate.
It mimics **GLP-1** with pride,
A hormone working deep inside.
It **slows the stomach**, tells the brain:
"You're full, don't eat"—again, again.
It also **boosts insulin release**,
When sugars rise, it brings some peace.
But Wegovy's goal is weight loss bold,
In patients where BMI takes hold.
Used for **chronic weight control**,
With diet, movement as the goal.
Given **once a week** by injection site,
**SubQ in abdomen**, thigh, or right.
Side effects? Let's name a few:
**Nausea, vomiting, diarrhea**, too.
**Constipation, fatigue, burping**, gassy—

Start low and slow, or things get sassy.

**Black box warning** must be said:

**Thyroid C-cell tumors** in rodent thread.

Avoid if **MEN2** is in their tree,

Or **medullary thyroid cancer** history.

Teach to **store in fridge**, keep it cool,

Inject the full dose, don't half the rule.

Rotate sites to keep skin clear,

And don't reuse the pen—keep it near.

No food required, any time,

But take it weekly on a dime.

And teach to call if vision blurs,

Or belly pain or faintness stirs.

Interactions? Just a few—

May delay **oral meds** passing through.

And when paired with **insulin** or a **sulfonylurea**,

The risk of **low sugar** gets a little drearier.

So Wegovy helps reduce the size,

With steady care and nurse-wise eyes.

With lifestyle change and weekly track,

It gives some patients their power back.

# Senna (Senokot, Ex-Lax)

*Stimulant Laxative – Bowel Motility Booster*

When bowels sleep and won't respond,
Senna gives a gentle prod.
A **stimulant laxative**, plant-derived,
It gets things moving, bowel revived.
It works on the **colon's muscle wall**,
By **stimulating nerves** to call.
Peristalsis starts to glide,
And stool begins its downward ride.
Used for **constipation**, short and mild,
Or in those **post-op** or **bedbound** filed.
Also paired in **bowel prep kits**,
To flush it clean before the scripts.
It kicks in **6 to 12 hours** slow,
So teach to take it **before bed's glow**.
By morning time, they'll feel the cue—
Just make sure a toilet's near and true.
Side effects? Nothing wild:
**Cramps**, **diarrhea**, may be styled.
**Discolored urine**—pink or brown—
Harmless but may cause a frown.

No black box, but caution still:
**Long-term use** may drain the will.
It can cause **dependence**, gut won't act,
Unless the senna's part of the pact.
Teach to use it **now and then**,
Not daily like a vitamin.
Hydration helps to make it kind,
Or cramping may not lag behind.
Pregnancy? Often still okay—
But ask the OB anyway.
And avoid in **bowel obstruction**,
Or **appendicitis** or sudden dysfunction
Often paired with **docusate**,
To soften *and* stimulate.
The combo's great for post-op strain,
To help prevent that pressure pain.
So Senna moves what's stuck inside,
With nurse-led care to safely guide.
Use it short, use it wise,
To help the gut mobilize.

# Sennosides/Docusate (Senna-S)

*Stimulant + Stool Softener Combo – Dual-Action Laxative*

When bowels need a nudge and slide,
Senna-S helps things move with pride.
A combo blend of **two in one**,
To get the job of pooping done.
**Sennosides** bring the muscle call,
A **stimulant** to the colon wall.
They trigger **peristalsis** strong,
So stool won't linger very long.

Then **docusate**—the softening star,
Draws in water from near and far.
It **moistens stool**, makes it smooth to pass,
So straining fades and movements last.
Used for **post-op**, **opioid clog**,
Or when they're backed up like a log.
Especially when the goal is clear:
Keep bowels soft but also near.

Side effects? A few to track:
**Cramps**, **diarrhea**, may circle back.

Too much use can bring **dependence**,
So short-term use is nurse-recommended.
No **black box warning**, but still take care—
Avoid in **obstruction** or **surgical scare**.
And teach them not to dose for days,
Unless the doc okay'd that phase.

Take it **at bedtime**, let it brew,
So morning brings the urge to do.
And remind them—**hydrate well**,
That's how this combo works so swell.
**Pregnancy-safe**, but still confirm,
In case their OB needs to affirm.
And don't mix it with **mineral oil**,
That combo's rough and might just spoil.

So Senna-S, a gentle tag team,
Helps bowels flow like a steady stream.
With nurse guidance and hydration plan,
It gets them going—yes, it can!

# Simethicone (Gas-X, Mylicon)

*Anti-Flatulent – Gas Relief Agent*

When bubbles bloat and pressure swells,
Simethicone breaks up the spells.
A gentle med, with one clear aim—
To pop the gas and ease the flame.
It works by **reducing surface tension**,
So gas bubbles lose their suspension.
They **combine and burst**, then float away,
So pressure, pain, and bloat don't stay.
Used for **gas, colic, post-op air**,
And **swallowed air** from eating flair.
In infants, kids, and adults too—
A safe, quick fix to get them through.
Side effects? Hardly seen.
It's one of the **safest meds** that's been.
No sedation, no GI strain,
Just gas relief without the pain.
No **black box warning**, no real scare,
Just teach to use it with some care.
Take it **after meals and before bed**,
To keep the bloating far ahead.

Can come in **chewables**, **drops**, or **gel**,
Or added to **antacids**, working well.
Shake the liquid, dose it right—
For infants, **Mylicon** calms the night.
No known drug interactions found,
It stays in gut—it won't go 'round.
Not absorbed, just passes through,
Doing what it's meant to do.
So Gas-X, Mylicon, simple relief,
Helps take the edge off gas and grief.
With nurse advice and patient cheer,
It makes the bloating disappear.

# Sodium Bicarbonate (Alka-Seltzer)

*Antacid / Alkalinizer – Acid Neutralizer & Gas Reliever*

When acid rises, hot and fast,
Sodium Bicarb helps it pass.
In fizzy tabs like **Alka-Seltzer**,
It brings relief that melts like shelter.
A **systemic antacid**, strong and quick,
It neutralizes acid thick.
Turns **HCl** into water and salt,
Easing heartburn's harsh assault.

Used for **indigestion**, **sour burn**,
And even in cases where acidosis returns.
Sometimes for **urine alkalization**, too,
Or in emergencies when pH is due.
Side effects? There are a few:
**Gas**, **bloating**, from $CO_2$.
**Sodium overload** is the fear—
So in **heart failure** patients, steer clear.

**Metabolic alkalosis** can arise,
If doses stack and kidneys compromise.

**Hypokalemia, tetany** signs—
So watch the labs for subtle lines.
No black box, but still be wise,
In **renal**, **cardiac**, or **edema** ties.
And **pregnancy**? Use with care,
High sodium might not play fair.

**Take it 1–3 hours post-meal**,
Or when heartburn tries to steal.
Dissolve the tab in water first,
Then sip it slowly—don't just burst.
Don't mix with **calcium or milk**,
Or risk a syndrome (alkali-milk!).
And space from other meds by time,
It can affect absorption's climb.

So Alka-Seltzer fizzes bright,
Relieves the burn and bloated fight.
With nurse-led tips and proper use,
It helps when acid runs too loose.

# Sodium Phosphate Enema (Fleet Enema)

*Osmotic Laxative – Rectal Bowel Evacuant*

When bowels block and won't respond,
Fleet Enema gives a prompt beyond.
A **hyperosmotic laxative**, clean and quick,
It pulls in water to move things slick.
It works by drawing fluid near,
Into the colon's lower sphere.
This softens stool and starts the squeeze,
To give that patient quick release.
Used for **constipation**, backed-up strain,
And **bowel prep** in the rectal lane.
Relief comes fast—**2 to 15 mins**,
So keep a toilet close for wins.
Side effects? Just a few:
**Cramping**, **rectal burning**, urgency too.
But bigger risks come if misused—
Especially if dosing is abused.
**Black box?** No, but here's the deal:
**Electrolyte shifts** are very real.

**Hyperphosphatemia, hypocalcemia,**
And **dehydration**—check that schema.
In **renal disease**, proceed with care,
The **phosphate load** can bring a scare.
**Elderly, heart failure,** or fragile folk—
Might need a different laxative poke.
Don't use it more than **once a day**,
And not for more than **three-day stay**.
Teach to **lubricate the tip**, go slow,
Insert while lying on left side low.
Encourage them to **hold it in**,
Until the urge begins to spin.
Then they can release with grace—
And ease the strain in bathroom space.
No systemic absorption is the goal,
But if retained too long, it takes a toll.
So patient teaching is key to do—
For safe, smooth outcomes all day through.
So Fleet Enema, fast and neat,
Brings on the bowel's final feat.
With nurse instruction and gentle tone,
It helps that stool get overthrown.

# Sofosbuvir (Sovaldi)

*Antiviral – NS5B Polymerase Inhibitor for Hepatitis C*

When Hep C lingers deep inside,
Sofosbuvir turns the tide.
A **direct-acting antiviral**, sleek,
It clears the virus in just a few weeks.
It targets **NS5B polymerase**,
An enzyme that Hep C needs to raise.
By blocking replication at its core,
It stops the virus from making more.
Used in combo—not alone,
With other meds like **Ledipasvir**, known.
For genotypes **1 through 4 or more**,
Depending on the patient's score.
**Cirrhosis?** Yes, it still may fit,
But dosing plans must carefully sit.
**With or without ribavirin** blends,
Sovaldi starts where healing sends.
Side effects? Pretty kind:
**Headache**, **fatigue**, **weakness** in mind.
**Nausea**, maybe **insomnia** seen,
But serious events are rare and lean.

No black box for Sovaldi's name,

But when combined—it's not the same.

**Ribavirin** brings risks to bear:

**Birth defects**, **anemia**, and more to spare.

And if combined with **amiodarone**,

**Bradycardia** could be full-blown.

So monitor pulse, and keep close eyes,

Especially when heart disease lies.

Take it **daily, same time each** day,

**With or without food**—either way.

But don't skip doses, keep it tight—

That's how you win the Hep C fight.

Teach to finish **every course**,

And come for labs with no remorse.

Watch **LFTs**, **HCV load**, and weight,

To track response and med relate.

So Sovaldi, small but bold in might,

Can lead Hep C into the night.

With nurse support and dosing wise,

It brings new hope where illness lies.

# Sucralfate (Carafate)

*GI Protectant – Mucosal Barrier Agent for Ulcers*

When ulcers sting and stomachs ache,
Sucralfate forms a healing lake.
A sticky shield, a soothing coat,
It wraps the wound just like a moat.
It's not an acid blocker type—
No pH change, no proton hype.
Instead, in acid's presence bright,
It forms a **paste that binds on site**.
Used for **duodenal ulcers**, mostly,
It clings to tissue warm and closely.
Also used off-label here
For **gastritis**, **GERD**, and mucosal repair.
It protects but doesn't absorb much—
It stays in the gut, just doing its touch.
So **side effects** are pretty tame:
**Constipation** is its most known name.
No black box warning—yay for that!
But interactions? Yep, there's that chat:
It **binds to other meds** like glue,
So space them out—**2 hours** will do.

Take it **on an empty stomach**, true,

**1 hour before meals**, then **at bedtime** too.

**Do not crush** the scored tablet form—

But **liquid** is fine for those who conform.

Don't take with **antacids** too near,

They block the acid it needs to adhere.

So **no aluminum overlap**,

Especially in **renal**—you'll dodge that trap.

Pregnancy? Safe, with guidance wise.

But always let the provider advise.

And tell them healing takes a span,

So keep the course—don't change the plan.

So Carafate brings comfort fast,

It shields the sore so healing lasts.

With nurse-led tips and proper pace,

It gives the gut a cozy place.

# Sulfasalazine (Azulfidine)

*Aminosalicylate / Anti-inflammatory – IBD & RA Agent*

When bowels flare with fire and pain,
Sulfasalazine soothes the strain.
An **aminosalicylate** combo blend,
With **anti-inflammatory** powers to lend.
It splits in the colon's lower part,
Releasing **5-ASA** to start.
It quiets the gut's immune cascade—
Where **ulcerative colitis** flares invade.
Used for **IBD**, and sometimes **RA**,
Though GI use leads the way.
It helps reduce the cramps and bleed,
By calming cytokine-driven speed.
Side effects? They're worth a glance:
**Nausea**, **headache**, **rash** by chance.
**Orange pee and skin** may show—
Harmless, but good for patients to know.
 Rare but risky, take this cue:
**SJS**, **hepatitis**, **bone marrow** too.
So **CBC**, **LFTs**, and **renal labs**
Should be routine on nurse-led tabs.

And don't forget the **sulfa tag**—
If allergic, this one's red-flag.
Also contains **salicylate**,
So use with caution, don't tempt fate.
**Take with food** to ease the gut,
And drink fluids to avoid a rut.
Can cause **crystalluria**, yes indeed—
So **hydration** is a vital need.
Teach them not to miss a dose,
And space it evenly, not close.
And don't stop suddenly—flare may wake,
So taper slow if breaks must take.
Can **reduce folate**, so give a boost,
**Folic acid** keeps red cells juiced.
Safe in pregnancy *if* cleared through,
But always let OB review.
So Sulfasalazine, bold and bright,
Helps cool the gut's inflammatory fight.
With steady labs and nursing care,
It brings IBD some long-lost air.

# Teduglutide (Gattex)

*GLP-2 Analog – Intestinal Growth & Nutrient Absorption for SBS*

When intestines lose their length or might,
Teduglutide helps them fight.
A **GLP-2 analog**, smart and rare,
It helps the gut repair with care.
It works by boosting **mucosal growth**,
In **short bowel syndrome** (that's the oath).
It enhances **absorption**, cell repair,
So nutrients linger, not vanish in air.

It **reduces need for IV feeds**,
By helping meet nutritional needs.
In those with **intestinal loss or disease**,
Gattex offers long-term ease.
**Subcutaneous injection**, daily dose,
Same time each day matters most.
Rotate sites, keep it clean,
And refrigerate to keep it keen.

Side effects? Let's take a peek:

**Abdominal pain, nausea, tooth issues** may speak.
**Injection site** redness, a common guest,
And **fluid overload** in some—so rest.
**Black box warning**—heads-up alert:
It may cause **colorectal cancer** to spurt.
So screen for **polyps** before they start,
And monitor with a cautious heart.

**GI obstruction, gallbladder flares**,
Or **pancreatitis**—watch for scares.
**Monitoring** is key throughout—
Liver tests, stools, and cancer doubts.
Teach to store it **in the fridge**,
Let it warm before you bridge.
And use **sterile technique** with care,
To minimize reaction flare.

So Gattex gives the gut new length,
Restores absorption, builds up strength.
With nurse-led teaching, labs, and track,
It helps bring nutrition back.

# Tegaserod (Zelnorm)

*5-HT4 Receptor Partial Agonist – Prokinetic for IBS-C (Women)*

When constipation slows the ride,
Tegaserod helps turn the tide.
As **Zelnorm**, it's a targeted friend,
For **IBS-C** where symptoms won't end.
It's a **partial agonist**, 5-HT4,
That gets the gut to move once more.
It boosts **motility**, **fluid flow**,
And helps those sluggish stools to go.

Approved for **women under 65**,
With **IBS-C**, it brings guts alive.
**Short-term use** is what it's for,
When diet and fiber just do no more.
Side effects? Some may arise:
**Diarrhea**, **gas**, or belly cries.
**Headache, back pain, abdominal strain**,
But mostly mild—and rarely remain.

**Black box once held its place,**

For **cardiac events** in a small-case trace.
It was pulled, then later cleared
For select use where risk's not feared.
So now it's back with safety screened—
**No heart history**, clean and gleaned.
No **stroke**, **MI**, or **angina's** past—
Or this med won't be a match.

Take it **before meals**, twice a day,
To help the bowels find their way.
**Discontinue** if symptoms stop
Or if side effects begin to pop.
No big drug interactions clash,
But still review the full med stash.
And avoid if kidneys fail,
Or liver labs begin to pale.

So Zelnorm helps the gut engage,
For women in the IBS-C stage.
With nurse-led care and patient trust,
It helps them poop when fiber won't adjust.

# Tenofovir (Viread)

*Nucleotide Reverse Transcriptase Inhibitor (NRTI) – Antiviral for Hep B & HIV*

When viruses hide inside the strand,
Tenofovir lends a steady hand.
As **Viread**, it's an NRTI,
That stops the virus from multiplying high.
It mimics DNA's building block,
Then **halts reverse transcriptase's clock**.
Used for **chronic Hepatitis B**,
And also **HIV**, selectively.
It helps suppress the viral load,
So liver damage doesn't explode.
Also part of **PrEP** and combo blends,
Where HIV prevention extends.
Side effects? Some worth the watch:
**GI upset**, **nausea**, **cramps**, and such.
**Headache, fatigue**, or **dizzy days**,
But most adjust in a few short stays.
**Black box warning** must be known:
**Lactic acidosis** has been shown.
Plus **hepatomegaly** with fatty streak—

So monitor liver every week.
And if **Hep B is suddenly stopped**,
**Acute flares** may come unblocked.
So don't discontinue on a whim—
It needs a plan that's not too slim.
Teach to take it **once per day**,
With or without food's okay.
But **stay on schedule**, never skip,
Or viral load could start to grip.
Check **renal labs**—this drug may strain
The **kidneys** in a slow, quiet chain.
**Bone density** may decline,
So **calcium**, **vitamin D**, and spine.
Pregnancy-safe with doctor lead,
But monitor both mom and seed.
And always use **with other meds**,
In HIV—it never treads
Alone, so teach about the stack
And never let adherence slack.
So Viread stands with power wide,
To fight Hep B and turn the tide.

# Ursodiol (Actigall, Urso Forte)

*Bile Acid – Gallstone Dissolver & Liver Support Agent*

When bile flows thick and stones take hold,

Ursodiol works calm and bold.

A **bile acid** made to match our own,

It helps dissolve what's overgrown.

Used to treat **gallstones** that don't need knife,

In patients who want to avoid the strife.

Also used for **PBC** care—

That's **primary biliary cholangitis** there.

It **reduces cholesterol** in bile,

Makes stones dissolve after a while.

It also keeps bile flowing smooth,

When ducts get scarred and lose their groove.

**Cytoprotective** for the liver cells,

It slows fibrosis where bile dwells.

A gentle nudge, not fast-acting fire,

But steady use is what we require

Side effects? Mostly mild:

**Diarrhea**, or gas beguiled.

**Headache**, **nausea**, some report,

But many find it's well-tolered support.

No black box warning, which is great—
But still, we check and calculate.
Not for those with **biliary block**,
Or **active gallbladder infection shock**.
Take it **with food**, divide the dose,
To help the gut absorb it close.
**Don't chew or crush**, let tablets glide,
With a glass of water at your side.
Treatment takes **months** or even a year,
So set expectations clear.
And follow up with **ultrasound**,
To see if stones are still around.
Monitor **LFTs** and CBCs,
To track how well the liver sees.
And teach the signs of gallstone pain—
RUQ aches that may remain.
So Ursodiol, slow but strong,
Helps the bile move right along.
With nurse support and patient trust,
It treats the liver without a fuss.

# Ustekinumab (Stelara)

*Monoclonal Antibody – IL-12/23 Inhibitor for IBD & Psoriasis*

When inflammation flares too high,
Stelara helps the storm pass by.
A **monoclonal antibody**, sleek and wise,
It calms the gut where trouble lies.
It blocks **interleukins 12 and 23**,
Cytokines that fuel disease.
By stopping them, it quiets the flame
In **Crohn's** and **ulcerative colitis**' name.
Also used for **psoriasis** skin,
And **psoriatic arthritis** flares within.
But in the GI world, it plays
A role in bringing calmer days.
Given first by **IV slow**,
Then **subcutaneously** to go.
**Every 8 weeks**, the dosing stands—
A steady rhythm in nurse hands.
Side effects? Let's review:
**Fatigue**, **headache**, and **injection site hue**.
**URI symptoms** like cough or throat,
And rare infections that take note.

No black box, but here's the scope:
**Serious infections** can still elope.
So screen for **TB** before you start,
And **monitor signs** that infection may dart.
**Malignancy risk** is low, but real,
So teach what symptoms might reveal.
And if they've got a **live vaccine**,
Hold off—Stelara dampens that scene.
No major interactions clash,
But **immunosuppressants**? Watch the stash.
Sometimes it's used as monotherapy,
To reduce immune activity.
Teach to **rotate injection sites**,
And store it cold, away from lights.
Don't shake the vial or warm too fast—
Be gentle, steady, and make it last.
So Stelara helps calm deep disease,
With dosing slow and steady ease.
With nurse support and teaching clear,
It brings relief and hope back near.

# Vancomycin Oral (Vancocin)

*Glycopeptide Antibiotic – C. difficile Infection Treatment*

When C. diff strikes with toxin load,
Vancomycin clears the colon road.
But this form's special—**oral** only here,
It **stays in the gut**, where bugs appear.
It's a **glycopeptide antibiotic**, strong,
Blocks **cell wall synthesis** all day long.
But unlike IV that spreads through veins,
This **oral form** stays in the drains
Used to treat **C. difficile colitis**,
When diarrhea turns to GI crisis.
For **severe or recurrent** flare,
It's the drug of choice with targeted care.
**No systemic absorption** in the gut,
So bloodstream effects? Not really a rut.
But in high doses or leaky GI,
Some **absorption** could sneak by.
Side effects? They're pretty tame:
**Nausea, cramping**, GI game.
But **resistance risk** is a concern,
So use it right and take your turn.

No **black box**, but let's be smart:

Monitor if kidney issues start.

More for **IV vanco**, to be fair,

But worth the watch if things impair.

Teach to **take it exactly timed**,

To keep those gut bugs realigned.

Even if they feel all better,

Finish the course down to the letter.

Watch for signs of **superinfection**,

Like yeast or new bug recollection.

And hydrate well—those stools are fast,

So fluids help their strength to last.

No big drug interactions known,

But always check before it's shown.

And **space from cholestyramine**,

It binds the drug before it's seen.

So oral Vanco, gut-specific cure,

Helps wipe out C. diff with effects so pure.

With nurse instruction, timing tight,

It brings the colon back to right.

# Vedolizumab (Entyvio)

*Integrin Receptor Antagonist – Gut-Selective Biologic for IBD*

When IBD won't calm or fade,
Vedolizumab joins the aid.
As **Entyvio**, it takes its stand—
A gut-specific helping hand.
It blocks **α4β7 integrin's gate**,
So immune cells pause before they hate.
It stops them from entering GI walls,
Reducing flares and painful calls.
Used for **ulcerative colitis**, **Crohn's** alike,
Especially when **TNF meds** strike
Out or cause too many woes—
This gut-selective option flows.
Given **IV infusion**, slow and neat:
**Week 0, 2, 6**, then every **8-week beat**.
No pre-meds usually needed here,
But monitor during, nurse stays near.
Side effects? Not too loud:
**Headache**, **joint pain**, tired crowd.
**Nausea**, **fever**, and maybe cough,
But usually it's well shrugged off.

No black box warning flash,

But **infections** can still make a splash.

So screen for **TB** before you start,

And hold it if they fall apart.

It's **gut-specific**, a major perk—

Less systemic immune work.

So fewer risks for widespread spread,

Compared to others in its thread.

No live vaccines while on the drip,

And report **new neuro symptoms** quick.

Though **PML** is very rare,

We still assess and stay aware.

Teach to stick to every date,

Even when they're feeling great.

Missing infusions can bring a flare,

So nursing reminders show we care.

So Entyvio helps calm the gut,

When Crohn's or UC makes life tough.

With infusion care and teaching guide,

It gives IBD a gentler ride.

# Vitamin B12 (Cyanocobalamin)

*Essential Water-Soluble Vitamin – Anemia & Nerve Support*

When energy drops and nerves feel strange,
B12 helps the body rearrange.
As **cyanocobalamin**, it fills the gap,
Where deficiency lays a weary trap.
It's key for **RBC formation's flow**,
And helps the **nervous system** glow.
It aids in **DNA repair**,
And keeps **methylation** running fair.

Used for **pernicious anemia's** call,
Or post-**gastrectomy**, when levels fall.
Also in **ileum disease** or **Crohn's**,
Where B12 loss has made its home.
Comes **oral, IM,** or **subQ,**
Or **nasal spray**—they'll choose with you.
IM's for those who can't absorb
Through GI tract that's been disturbed.

Side effects? They're very few:
**Injection site pain,** maybe **headache,** too

Rarely **hypokalemia** appears
As red cells flood in early years.
No black box warning—safe and sound,
But still, some rules must go around.
Teach that **lifelong therapy** may apply,
In **autoimmune loss** or gut gone awry.

Monitor **CBC**, **B12**, and more,
Check **methylmalonic acid** to be sure.
Watch for signs of neuro strife—
**Tingling**, **gait change**, or "brain fog" life.
Taken **with food**, oral is fine,
But high-dose may be by design.
And if the cause is malabsorption's weight,
Injections may just work great.

So B12 brings the spark back in,
To boost red cells and help nerves win.
With nurse advice and steady track,
It puts the body's power back.

**for getting this book and for making it all the way to the end!**

Before you go, I wanted to ask you for one small favor. Could you please consider posting a review? Because posting a review is the best and easiest way to support the work of independent authors like me.

Your feedback will help me a ton!

Click **Here** or Scan the QR code below!

# OTHER TITLES IN THE MADE EASY SERIES

Geriatrics Made Easy
Emergency Care Made Easy
Critical Care Made Easy
Human Growth & Development
Maternal & Newborn Made Easy
Mental Health Made Easy
Organic Chemistry Made Easy
General Chemistry Made Easy
Pediatrics Made Easy
Med-Surg Made Easy, Vol 1
Med-Surg Made Easy, Vol 2
Microbiology Made Easy
Nursing Skills & Procedures
Pathophysiology Made Easy
Nursing Assessment Made Easy
Nutrition Made Easy
Anatomy & Physiology Vol 1
Anatomy & Physiology Vol 2

## Pharmacology Series
Pharmacology Made Easy Vol 1
Pharmacology Made Easy Vol 2
Pharmacology Made Easy Vol 3
Oncology Meds Made Easy
Cardiac Meds Made Easy
Endocrine Meds Made Easy
Pain Meds Made Easy
GI Meds Made Easy
Respiratory Meds Made Easy
Critical Meds Made Easy
ER/ICU Meds Made Easy
Neuro Meds Made Easy
Psych Meds Made Easy
Pediatric Meds Made Easy
OB/GYN Meds Made Easy

www.ingramcontent.com/pod-product-compliance
Lightning Source LLC
Chambersburg PA
CBHW052151220526
45471CB00004B/1634